Take this
Word to Heart

Take this Word to Heart

The Shema in Torah and Gospel

Perry B. Yoder, editor

Contributors:
Jackie A. Wyse
James W. Carlson
Jeff T. Williams
Amy Barker

Occasional Papers, No. 23

Institute of Mennonite Studies
Elkhart, Indiana

Co-published with Herald Press
Scottdale, Pennsylvania
Waterloo, Ontario

Copyright © 2005 by Institute of Mennonite Studies
3003 Benham Avenue, Elkhart, Indiana 46517-1999
www.ambs.edu/IMS

Co-published with Herald Press
616 Walnut Avenue, Scottdale, Pennsylvania 15683
490 Dutton Drive, Unit C8, Waterloo, Ontario N2L 6H7
www.heraldpress.com

Printed in Canada by Pandora Press, Kitchener, Ontario
Institute of Mennonite Studies ISBN 0-936273-38-0

Library of Congress Cataloging-in-Publication Data

Take this word to heart : the Shema in Torah and Gospel / Perry B.
Yoder, editor.
    p. cm.
  ISBN 0-936273-38-0 (alk. paper)
  1. God—Worship and love—Biblical teaching. 2. Shema. I. Yoder,
Perry B.
  BV4817.T35 2005
  231'.6—dc22
                            2005013820

Cover design by Mary E. Klassen
Calligraphy by Rosanna E. McFadden

Contents

Foreword

The best teachers never stop learning. They have developed disciplines of mind and heart that nourish a sense of wonder. They pursue the subject of their passion with vision and purpose. When they muster the courage to offer their gift of great things to students as work in progress, the ensuing interaction creates a learning community.[1] At the heart of this encounter, a transformation takes place. Gathered for a common purpose, students and teacher create an outcome which is something greater than the sum of its parts.

The title of this unassuming volume, *Take this Word to Heart*, paraphrases the self-referential admonition of Moshe Rabbenu (Moses, Our Teacher) in Deuteronomy 6:4–5. "Hear, O Israel" is both a command and an invitation. So, too, the master teacher entangles the students in a web of compulsion and enticement. New material must be mastered, assignments completed, perhaps even tests taken. And certainly there are papers to be written. But there is also the promise of buried treasure. "Here is a word that has spoken to me," says the teacher. "It is my hope that it will also speak to you. And if you take this word to heart, it will speak to me anew through your discoveries."

The works collected in this volume are the product of the 2002 Biblical Studies Seminar at Associated Mennonite Biblical Seminary. Each makes a unique contribution to our understanding of the Shema. Taken together, the essays give voice to a deeply shared journey of

---

[1] See Parker Palmer, *The Courage to Teach: Exploring the Inner Landscape of a Teacher's Life* (San Francisco: Jossey-Bass, 1998), especially chapter 4, "Knowing in Community: Joined by the Grace of Great Things."

discovery. Having studied this passage together, the authors explore in their own papers different themes or aspects of its origins, development, and meaning. In making the results of this study available to a broader audience through publication, their learning is extended to other classrooms and to members of the community of faith who will use it in congregational Bible study and benefit from its insights.

There is a popular misconception of the rarified atmosphere of the graduate seminar as the sterile launching ground of esoteric papers, as countless as they are pointless. The vigor and passion of these essays should help correct this false image. These essays not only illustrate the kinds of work that graduate students in Bible and theology do and the methods they employ, but they also represent an accessible resource for those interested in biblical interpretation in general and the Shema in particular. Regardless of how much of the philological and literary analysis the reader is able to follow, one thing that emerges clearly from these studies is the importance of contexts for understanding scripture. The chapters explore in turn the literary, thematic, theological, and historical contexts that are a crucial prerequisite for understanding the moral imperative of the Shema.

This book also provides eloquent testimony to the fact that biblical exegesis done well is necessarily intertestamental. That Jesus himself was rooted in the faith and scripture of Judaism is a theological truism for Christians—and yet one often ignored in practice. We continue to bear the burden of a long, shameful history of Christian anti-Semitism, in our attitudes as well as our behaviors. At the center of our faith, and of our interpretation of the Bible, is Jesus Christ. The proper context for understanding Jesus' life and teachings is the scripture that shaped his own community of faith.

Finally, this set of essays on the Shema reinforces the fundamental truth that in biblical religion, worship and ethics are deeply interdependent. Although each may be treated as a separate domain, with a self-justifying logic and purpose, taking the words of scripture to heart entails living out the justice and mercy of its teachings. It is no surprise that the command/invitation of Jesus to his followers to take up his cross and follow him daily in life reflects the ethos of his favorite Bible passage.

I invite you to read this book, and to take its words to heart.

Paul Keim

Introduction

Perry B. Yoder

What is the most important verse in the Bible? Some would say John 3:16, a verse many memorize in childhood. Others might choose Paul's response to the Philippian jailor: "Believe on the Lord Jesus, and you will be saved" (Acts 16:31). If asked instead, "What was the most important verse in the Bible for Jesus?" we might well identify his reply to a similar question: "The first is, 'Hear, O Israel: the Lord our God, the Lord is one; you shall love the Lord your God with all your heart, and with all your soul, and with all your mind, and with all your strength'" (Mark 12:29-30).

Jesus in quoting Deuteronomy 6:4-5 was citing perhaps the central verse for Jews of his day. This passage was part of what was known as the Shema, after its initial word in Hebrew, שְׁמַע (hear). In the other two synoptic Gospels (Matt. 22:37; Luke 10:27), only Deuteronomy 6:5 is quoted. Mark alone includes Deuteronomy 6:4. Although this text was central for Jesus, it is quoted differently in each of these three Gospels.

Given the primacy of this verse for Jesus and for other Jews, some questions come immediately to mind. First, what was the meaning of these verses in Deuteronomy, and when did they become central for Jewish faith? Second, why do the synoptic Gospels quote this verse differently? One might expect, given the centrality of the passage, that they would agree on its formulation. In fact, even the question to which Jesus is responding varies: In Luke, Jesus is asked, "What must I do to inherit eternal life?" while in Matthew and Mark the question is, "Which commandment in the law is the greatest?" (or, "Which commandment is the first of all?"). Moreover, in Luke it is not Jesus but Jesus' questioner who gives the answer! Surely if Deuteronomy 6:4-5 is the most important text in the Bible for Jesus, we might expect more agreement on question and answer, and about who quoted the verse.

Because of the fundamental importance of the Shema, and because of the perplexity raised by its varied forms in the Synoptics, students in the spring 2002 Biblical Studies Seminar at Associated Mennonite Biblical Seminary (Elkhart, Indiana) devoted themselves to a study of the Shema. Each of the four students in the seminar focused attention on one of four passages: Deuteronomy 6:4–9 and its different appropriation in each of the synoptic Gospels. This book documents the results of their work. These essays are rich in insights and will, I am confident, spark readers' interest and imagination.

I have described the Shema as central to Jewish faith. The phrase *Jewish faith* sounds strange because it is commonplace to describe Judaism as centering on practice (orthopraxis), rather than on belief (orthodoxy). For example, in his classic work, *Judaism in the First Centuries of the Christian Era*, George Foot Moore notes the lack of schism within rabbinic Judaism until the time of the Karaites in the eighth century. He proposes that "the ground of this remarkable unity is to be found not so much in a general agreement in fundamental ideas as in community of observance.... Wherever a Jew went he found the same system of domestic observance in effect."[1] In this "domestic effect" Moore includes dietary laws and the synagogue service, with its prayers and recitation of the Shema. He concludes, "This unity and universality ... was not based upon orthodoxy in theology but upon uniformity of observance."[2]

In a similar way, Leo Baeck writes of an ethical monotheism that he considers the basis of Israel's monotheism. It is encapsulated in the Shema. The result of this monotheism is that "in Judaism to know God does not imply an understanding of the nature of His Being but a knowledge of His government, a perception of and an effort to follow the right way, the way which God has revealed and which is the same for all types of human beings."[3]

---

[1] George Foote Moore, *Judaism in the first Centuries of the Christian Era* (Cambridge, MA: Harvard University Press, 1927–1930), 1:110. On the history of the Karaites and the lack of sectarian schism in Judaism, see more recently Nathan Shur, *Toldot ha-Kara'im* (Jerusalem: Mosad Byalik, 2003).

[2] Moore, *Judaism*, 111.

[3] Leo Baeck, "Morality as a Basic Requirement of Judaism," in *The Foundations of Jewish*

It is not that Jews did not do philosophy and theology; philosophers and theologians such as Sa'adia Gaon and Maimonides were widely influential. Maimonides' influence extended to Thomas Aquinas and Christian theology. But, as Menachen Kellner puts it, "The whole project of creed formulation is basically alien to biblical-rabbinic Judaism,"[4] because rabbinic Judaism "did not define a Jew in terms of his beliefs." Consequently, "personal salvation . . . is not dependent upon orthodoxy in the strict sense of the term . . . but upon submission to the will of God as expressed in the commandments of the Torah."[5] Judaism was not a creedal religion, and no creedal statement marked one's Jewish identity.

In light of this widely held view that Judaism depends on orthopraxis (right behavior) rather than on orthodoxy (right belief), what is the role of theological claims in Judaism? What is the place of the Shema, in particular, which confesses the most basic belief of monotheism, that God is one?

Moshe Weinfeld has written about Decalogue and the Recitation of "Shema": The Development of the Confessions. He begins the book with the claim that "these two documents constitute, each in its own way, what may be termed a credo in the broad sense of the term."[6] This claim rests on the daily practice of reciting the Ten Commandments and the Shema in the Second Temple period, and the development within the biblical tradition of the Ten Commandments as a unique literary unit. What is intriguing and significant in his thesis is the early date at which these two texts served as core statements of belief. Noteworthy also is the connection between the Shema and the Ten Commandments, which may be signaled already by their proximity in Deuteronomy 5 and 6. This connection would seem to indicate an early notion that the Shema, the affirmation concerning God, needed to be accompanied by a similar affirmation concerning ethics.

Ethics, vol. 1 of The Teachings of Judaism, comp. Simon Bernfeld, trans. Armin Hajman Koller (New York: Macmillan, 1929), 17–18.

[4] Menachem Marc Kellner, Dogma in Medieval Jewish Thought: From Maimonides to Abravanel (Oxford: Oxford University Press, 1986), 1.

[5] Ibid, 2.

[6] Moshe Weinfeld, Aseret ha-dibrot u-keri'at Shema: gilgulehen shel hats'harot emunah (Tel Aviv: ha-Kibuts ha-me'uhad, 2001). Title as translated on the copyright page.

Weinfeld's contention that these two texts served a creedal function early in the history of Judaism is at odds with Gerhard von Rad's argument concerning Israel's credo. Von Rad claimed that the recital of history was the Israelite credo. In Deuteronomy 26, for example, the worshiper offering the first fruits of the land recites a summary of Israel's history. The act of the worshiper was a response to the events of grace recited in this "creed." Such a recital of historical events as a creed used in worship contrasts with latter Christian creeds, which were much more abstract and "theological."[7] Von Rad's has been the usual notion in Old Testament studies: the creed of Israelite religion, if such a creed existed, was based on historical narrative, not theological statement.

In terms of endurance and liturgical use within the Jewish community, Weinfeld seems to have the better argument. The Nash Papyrus, from about 150 BCE, contains the Exodus 20 version of the Decalogue, followed by Deuteronomy 6:4–5; it thus provides evidence that the Decalogue and the Shema were already combined in the second century BCE. Later supporting evidence is the pattern of daily recitation in the temple of the Decalogue and the Shema.

In the Dead Sea Scrolls we find evidence of the "greater" Shema, that is, the Shema in Deuteronomy 6 combined with material from Deuteronomy 11 and Numbers 15. This selection of texts became known in Jewish liturgy as the Shema proper. Although not connected at Qumran with the Decalogue, this material was already used liturgically there.[8]

According to the Mishnah, written in the late second century but containing older traditions, the complete reading of the Shema was to take place twice daily. In the morning, two benedictions were pronounced before the recitation of the Shema and one afterward. In the evening, two benedictions preceded and two followed the Shema. But

---

[7] See his essay, "The Form-Critical Problem of the Hexateuch," for the development of this thesis (in *The Problem of the Hexateuch and other Essays*, trans. E. W. Trueman Dicken [Edinburgh: Oliver & Boyd, 1966]; originally published as *Gesammelte Studien zum Alten Testament* [Munich: Kaiser Verlag, 1958]).

[8] See Esther Eshel, "4QDeut^n—A Text That Has Undergone Harmonistic Editing," *Hebrew Union College Annual* 62 (1991), ed. Herbert H. Paper (Cincinnati: Hebrew Union College, 1992), 117–54.

we do not find mention of the Ten Commandments accompanying the recitation of the Shema.[9]

What is evident from this brief discussion of the evolution of the recitation of the Shema is that Deuteronomy 6:4 seems to have been accompanied by other scriptural material; the "simple" Shema of Deuteronomy 6:4 did not stand alone. At times it was accompanied by the Decalogue and was expanded to include other related passages from Deuteronomy 11 and Numbers 15. Also, by the time of the New Testament, Deuteronomy 6:4 apparently was a well-known liturgical and confessional element, perhaps along with the passages from Deuteronomy and Numbers and perhaps in combination with the Decalogue. It is significant that at an early time, the Shema was sometimes coupled with the ethical material of the Decalogue.

Even as the composition of the Shema has undergone change in the course of its historical development, so the understanding of its first verse has varied. Compare, for example, "Hear, O Israel: The LORD our God is one LORD" (RSV), with "Hear, O Israel: The LORD is our God, the LORD alone" (NRSV). This difference in interpretation reaches at least back into the Middle Ages. What is being confessed: the unity of God or the uniqueness of God? This issue of interpretation remains a point of discussion among modern commentators.

In the first essay below, Jackie Wyse discusses Deuteronomy 6:4–9. She begins with the exegesis of the Shema and then surveys how other scholars have related this passage to its context in Deuteronomy. She then presents her own suggestion of how the Shema functions in its Deuteronomic context. After a thorough contextualization of the unit in its literary setting, she returns to fine-tune her opening discussion of the interpretation of the Shema. She concludes by suggesting an understanding of this confession that is informed and enriched by its present literary context and function in Deuteronomy.

Wyse's paper is an admirable display of literary and theological reading. To it we may add another dimension by seeing Deuteronomy 6:4 in its wider historical or intellectual context. Eckart Otto, who has published prolifically on biblical and ancient Near Eastern law, suggests that Deuteronomy represents a reaction to Assyrian political theory

---

[9] See *m. Ber.*

and practice.[10] Understanding Deuteronomy against the backdrop of the neo-Assyrian treaties is not new, but Otto places the book in a new light by seeing it as a political manifesto directed against Assyrian demands for ultimate political loyalty.

On the basis of an Assyrian coronation hymn, VAT 13831, Assurbanipal's Coronation Hymn, Otto argues that the Assyrian king being described as the "image of " Aššur, the divine king of all the gods, represented Aššur on earth. Thus Assurbanipal, the king, could demand absolute loyalty from all his subjects.[11] According to Otto, Deuteronomy marks the transfer of absolute loyalty from the Assyrian king, the image of Aššur, not to the Judean king but to God alone.[12] Against this background, the Shema becomes not only a theological statement but a political statement. It is a confession of a loyalty to God that transcends loyalty to any earthly regime or power. This confession denies ultimate loyalty to the Assyrian king and to the Judean king as well.

When we come to the synoptic Gospels, we are immediately faced with two obvious questions. First, why is it only in Mark that the Shema proper actually occurs? That is, only in Mark do we find the citation beginning with Deuteronomy 6:4, "Hear, O Israel . . ." Why do Matthew and Luke omit this verse? All would expect the quote to begin with Deuteronomy 6:4, because the Shema began thus in the temple liturgy

---

[10] Otto writes, "The Neo-Assyrian period of the eight and seventh century BCE was the first decisive phase in the literary formation of the Hebrew Bible. The book of Deuteronomy as a counter-programme to the Assyrian state ideology enlightened the antagonism of divergent ideas of what a state should be" (Eckart Otto, "Human Rights: The Influence of the Hebrew Bible," *Journal of Northwest Semitic Languages* 25 [1999]: 4. See Otto's bibliography there).

[11] Ibid., 10. Otto quotes the text in his article. For its publication, see Alasdair Livingstone, *Court Poetry and Literary Miscellanea* (Helsinki: Helsinki University Press, 1989), 26–27.

[12] See Eckart Otto, *Krieg und Frieden in der Hebräischen Bibel und im Alten Orient: Aspekte für eine Friedensordnung in der Moderne* (Stuttgart: W. Kohlhammer, 1999), 86–91, for further argumentation. There he writes, "The recent notion of the limitation of state power by the authority of a God who demands absolute loyalty was also the fruit of the tradition history of the Hebrew Bible, more precisely, [the fruit] of the debate of Jewish intellectuals with the loyalty claims of the Assyrian hegemonic power" (86). The result of this debate was that loyalty to the emperor is transferred to YHWH when withdrawn from the Assyrian king; this shift of power from the king to God "fundamentally changed the legitimacy of royal power and thereby the function of the king" (91; my translation).

and in individual prayer. Indeed, it is this verse that contains the central confession of loyalty to God alone.

The second intriguing question is the origin of the pairing of the Shema with the love command found in Leviticus 19:18. This close pairing of the two great commandments has been found explicitly only in the teaching of Jesus. Is this pairing an innovation for Jesus, or was he reminding his audience of their religious tradition? These two questions form the point of departure for the three papers on the Synoptics.

James Carlson tackles the occurrence of the Shema in Mark 12:28–34. His point of entry is a discussion of Mark's audience. Does the writer begin with the Shema itself—"Hear, O Israel ..."—because the Gospel is addressed to a Gentile audience, as many commentators argue? On the basis of a careful exegesis of the language in Mark and a consideration of the possible contexts for this Gospel, Carlson's conclusion is different from this regnant hypothesis. He proposes that this formulation of the "greatest commandment" begins with Deuteronomy 6:4 because Mark's Gospel is addressed to a Hellenistic Jewish audience.

Jeff Williams discusses the Shema as it occurs in Luke 10:25–28. Here the unusual formulation of the commandment catches the eye. It is formulated as a single commandment—you shall love God and neighbor. What is the origin of or reason for this unique formulation? Williams first traverses the usual territory. Is Luke perhaps recasting the language he found in Mark for a specific purpose? Or might it be that Luke follows a different recension of the material as already found in Q? In that case, the difference would be the product of his tradition, his source, rather than being attributable to his own authorship.

But is there really only a single command here? Many scholars have argued for an ellipsis of the second verb and have therefore contended that this reformulation by Luke is not significant. Williams disagrees and makes a compelling argument for the significance of Luke's text, on the basis of the first-century setting and the text's function within its Lukan context, Luke 10:25–37. In short, Williams contends, the reformulation is real, and it does have significance.

Williams addresses yet another divergence from the Markan form of the command. In Luke, Jesus does not state the command; his interlocutor does so. Here the narrative is cast as a testing story. In a testing story, typically someone presents Jesus with a question, a test, and Jesus answers. In Luke 10, however, Jesus defers the question, and the answer is placed in the mouth of the lawyer who posed the question.

What does this change in speaker imply for our understanding of the Shema in Luke? Williams argues that the shift in speaker shifts the emphasis to the second part of the command, love for neighbor.

In the final essay, Amy Barker begins her study with a careful examination of how the Shema and love command are cited in Matthew. The larger point in her study, however, is to demonstrate that the double command in Matthew serves as Jesus' central hermeneutical principle.

The focus of her paper, then, is to show that for Matthew—and for Jesus, in Matthew's depiction—the double love command is a central hermeneutical principle that holds together the old and the new, the Torah and the new Jesus movement. Barker further suggests that this function of the second love command in Matthew, love for one's neighbor, represents a significantly different point of view than does this command in Paul, as cited in Romans 13:9. In Romans 13, obeying the love command fulfills the law, but it was not so with Matthew.

Barker points to the puzzling fact that the Shema is never quoted in the New Testament outside the synoptic Gospels. It may be alluded to in statements about the oneness or uniqueness of God, but it is not quoted as in the Synoptics. Instead it is the love command, Leviticus 19:18, that is picked up and cited frequently in the New Testament.[13] How might this phenomenon be explained?

It can safely be presumed that the early church and the other New Testament writers both knew the Shema and held to its validity. It was a commonplace in their religious environment, at least for the Jewish Christians who formed the original church. Perhaps it is not quoted because it was held in common with the Judaisms of the time. We might argue that it was the love command that became a significant point of departure for the early church. However, the political implication, the confession of loyalty to God that transcends loyalty to any earthly ruler, is still in evidence. As Peter and the apostles assert, "We must obey God rather than any human authority" (Acts 5:29). God's claim stands above all human claims.

In trying to forge a new ethic for a people of faith that soon became a mixture of Palestinian Jews, Diaspora Jews, and Gentiles, the

---

[13] See Pheme Perkins, *Love Commands in the New Testament* (New York: Paulist Press, 1982), for an overview of how and where the love command is used.

early church certainly made attempts to hold together the Hebrew scriptures and what was new in nascent Christianity. Paul argued that the foundation should, at least, not be laid using the identity markers of Jewish law such as circumcision and kosher food.

Within first-century Judaisms, Paul was in good company in arguing that not all of the Torah applied to Gentiles. The law was for Jews, given to them at Mount Sinai, and intended only in part for Gentiles. Certain regulations may apply to the Gentiles, but these people need not become Jews or keep the Jewish law.[14] But what should be done with Gentiles who became Christians? Was it acceptable that they remain Gentile, or must they first convert to Judaism?

The prevalence of the love command in the New Testament would seem to indicate that Jesus, by pairing the Shema with Leviticus 19:18, gave it enduring status for the Christian community. It may not be too much to claim that this command became a hallmark of early Christian ethics and defining for the character of the early church.

---

[14] See Klaus Müller, *Tora für die Völker: Die noachidischen Gebote und Ansätze zu ihrer Rezeption im Christentum*, 2nd ed. (Berlin: Institut Kirche und Judentum, 1998).

CHAPTER ONE

Loving God as an act of obedience: The Shema in context

Jackie A. Wyse

A midrashic legend describes a fanciful origin for the Shema.[1] Thought to have come from Rabbi Akiba in the late first or early second century, this early Tannaitic midrash on the book of Deuteronomy understands the word "Israel" in the Shema's opening declaration to refer to Jacob. The midrash chronicles Jacob's worries about the paths his children will choose, worries that haunt him until he is "about to depart from this world."[2] At that time, Jacob calls his sons to him, reproves them each individually, and then asks them the question of all questions: "Do you have any doubts concerning Him who spoke, and the world came into being?"[3] To Jacob's relief and delight, his sons respond in the best possible way—they recite the Shema: "Hear, O Israel, our father! Just as you have no doubts about Him who spoke, and the world came into being, so do we have no doubts. Rather, the Lord, our God, the Lord is one." Jacob is reassured about his family's future, and God's response is telling: "Jacob, surely this is what you desired all your days—that your children should recite the Shema morning and evening."[4]

---

[1] *Sipre*, 31. For text and translation, see Reuven Hammer, *Sifre: A Tannaitic Commentary on the Book of Deuteronomy*, Yale Judaica Series 24 (New Haven: Yale University Press, 1986).

[2] Although Reuben came dangerously close to fulfilling Jacob's fears, this text sees him as excused for his incestuous transgression because of his truly repentant spirit.

[3] Throughout this essay, I retain the masculine pronoun in quotations from ancient texts.

[4] Hammer, *Sifre*, 58.

Thus, a spontaneous proclamation of God's sovereignty was transformed into a daily discipline, anchoring Jacob's hopes for his progeny in the nature of God. As Reuven Hammer points out, Akiba "succeeded in creating a meaning for the Shema which would connect it not only to the majestic but abstract theological act of the acceptance of God's kingship . . . but [also] to the human story of a father and his anxiety for his family, a microcosm of the eternal concern of the Jewish people for its sons and daughters." The Shema is presented as an "act of family loyalty" as well as a liturgical and theological declaration of God's reign.[5] This legendary account gives the Shema primacy by rooting it in one of the Pentateuch's most ancient narratives. The Shema is depicted as older than Moses and Sinai—older even than the Decalogue, which is perhaps the only text in the Hebrew Bible rivaling the Shema in significance.

Although midrashic treatments of the origin of Jewish prayers are common, scholars acknowledge this midrash as one of supreme artistry.[6] What is the Shema, that it inspired such a well-crafted tale? How do we estimate the importance of this text, whose syllables have graced the lips of devout Jews at least twice daily for centuries, whose phrases have long been lauded by devout Christians and their Gospel writers as the "greatest" commandment? An investigation into the meaning of the Shema must precede answers to such questions. As we shall see, this text makes a daring pronouncement about the identity of YHWH before commissioning Israel to love YHWH with all that is theirs. The literary and historical contexts of the Shema will further elucidate the Shema's exhortation to love YHWH, shedding light on the relationship between loving YHWH and obeying YHWH's commands.

THE TEXT OF THE SHEMA

Commonly, Deuteronomy 6:4–9 is given the name *Shema*,[7] although occasionally this title is reserved for verses 4–5 alone. During the first

---

[5] Reuven Hammer, "A Legend concerning the Origins of the Shema," *Judaism* 32 (1983): 51, 55.

[6] Ibid., 51.

[7] Michael Wyschogrod writes that "the Talmudic rabbis always saw [Deut. 6:4–9] as a unit" ("The 'Shema Israel' in Judaism and the New Testament," in *The Roots of our Common Faith: Faith in the Scriptures and in the Early Church*, Faith and Order Paper 119, ed. Hans-Georg Link [Geneva: World Council of Churches, 1984], 23).

few centuries of the Common Era, as the Shema became a more firmly established part of Jewish liturgy, Deuteronomy 6:4–9 was more and more often paired with two other texts, Deuteronomy 11:13–21 and Numbers 15:37–41. Following the conventions of Jewish liturgics, this entire group of texts was called by the name of the first: the Shema. Even today, when Jews speak of praying the Shema, they usually refer to these three texts prayed in succession. In this study, however, the term *Shema* will refer to Deuteronomy 6:4–9 only.

The Shema can be divided into three portions, each with its own linguistic and syntactic challenges. The first part, Deuteronomy 6:4, is as follows:

שְׁמַע יִשְׂרָאֵל	Hear, O Israel:
יְהוָה אֱלֹהֵינוּ	The LORD is our God,
יְהוָה אֶחָד׃	the LORD alone.[8]

The first two words are translated easily enough. The word שְׁמַע, in its imperative form, connotes obedient listening. The phrase as a whole, שְׁמַע יִשְׂרָאֵל, is widely thought to serve as an introductory phrase "focusing [one's] attention" on the teaching that follows.[9] However, the final four words have for centuries been the subject of intense and frequent debate among scholars. The controversy boils down to two basic questions: First, does יְהוָה אֱלֹהֵינוּ יְהוָה אֶחָד in verse 4 constitute one clause or two? Second, what is the meaning of the word אֶחָד—"one" or "alone"? The answers to these two questions (which will be explored in this essay's conclusion) are of great significance, because 6:4 offers foundational knowledge about the identity of the God whom readers are instructed to love without reservation.

The Shema's second portion, Deuteronomy 6:5, reads:

וְאָהַבְתָּ אֵת יְהוָה אֱלֹהֶיךָ	You shall love the LORD your God
בְּכָל־לְבָבְךָ	with all your heart,
וּבְכָל־נַפְשְׁךָ	and with all your soul,
וּבְכָל־מְאֹדֶךָ׃	and with all your might.

[8] Except where noted, all English translations of scripture are taken from the New Revised Standard Version (NRSV).

[9] Jeffrey H. Tigay, *Deuteronomy: The Traditional Hebrew Text with the New JPS Translation,* The JPS Torah Commentary (Philadelphia: Jewish Publication Society, 1996), 76.

Deuteronomy 6:6, beginning the Shema's third portion, extends the enigma of loving Yhwh.

וְהָי֞וּ הַדְּבָרִ֣ים הָאֵ֗לֶּה   These words
אֲשֶׁ֨ר אָנֹכִ֧י מְצַוְּךָ֛ הַיּ֖וֹם   which I am commanding you today
עַל־לְבָבֶֽךָ   are upon your heart.[10]

In this verse, the words Yhwh is commanding you (מְצַוְּךָ) are upon your heart (לְבָבֶךָ). The term "heart" (לְבָבֶךָ) links this verse to the one directly before it, reminding the reader of the injunction to love Yhwh with all of one's heart. "Command" (מְצַוְּךָ) situates the Shema within the larger contexts of Yhwh's commands and human obedience—themes that recur not only in chapters 4 and 5 but throughout the book of Deuteronomy. The remaining three verses of the Shema offer concrete methods for making sure Yhwh's words remain upon one's heart, where they belong: the instruction of children; the recitation of Yhwh's words when at home and when away from home, during the day and at night; and the fashioning of reminders of Yhwh's all-important words.

Thus, the Shema comes to us entangled with questions about the identity of Yhwh, the human calling to love Yhwh, and the possibility of connecting human love for Yhwh with the words and commands of Yhwh. Before examining the linguistic and syntactic challenges of the Shema in greater detail, we must determine and examine the passage's larger literary context. Just as a jeweler considers the setting of a diamond in assessing its character, so we may gain insight into the character of the Shema by appraising the gems that surround it.

The Shema's Literary Context: Two Approaches

A variety of opinions exist regarding the boundaries of the Shema's immediate literary context. Here, I will present the views of Moshe Weinfeld and Michael Wyschogrod and then offer a third possibility for consideration.

In his commentary on Deuteronomy, Weinfeld argues that the Shema's immediate literary context is Deuteronomy 6:4–25. He breaks this larger section into four pericopes. The first is Deuteronomy 6:4–5, which Weinfeld calls "a declaration of faith" that provides "a theoreti-

---

[10] My translation. The NRSV renders this sentence more freely, "Keep these words that I am commanding you today in your heart."

cal restatement of the first two commandments of the Decalogue: the unity of God corresponds to the first commandment, while the denial of all other divinities corresponds to the second."[11] (In this way, Weinfeld maintains that God's unity and God's uniqueness are invoked in Deuteronomy 6:4.)[12] The second pericope is Deuteronomy 6:7–9, a "didactic passage," while the third is 6:10–19, which Weinfeld dubs "a homily . . . with references to the Decalogue."[13] Deuteronomy 6:20–25 forms the fourth pericope, another didactic section, exhorting the reader "to teach successive generations the great deeds of the Exodus, thus motivating the observance of the laws."[14] Weinfeld views the first pericope (6:4–5) as the introduction to a "great homily" which does not conclude until 11:32, while the second and fourth pericopes (6:7–9 and 6:20–25) "serve in fact as a frame for the [smaller] homily," that is, the third pericope (6:10–19).[15] The second and fourth pericopes are united by their commitment to catechism, the concern for passing down the creedal traditions faithfully to successive generations. It seems appropriate for these two passages to frame the homily in 6:10–19 because the homily's subject matter is largely based on the themes of the Exodus, the promise of land, and (as Weinfeld points out) the importance of keeping the Decalogue—traditions that Jewish families are expected to teach their children, and Jewish rabbis, their students.

Michael Wyschogrod offers another option for the Shema's larger literary context. Rather than connecting the Shema with the verses after it, Wyschogrod links it with preceding verses, arguing that Deuteronomy 5:1–6:9 forms a single message—a single speech of Moses.[16] The climax of this unit, according to Wyschogrod, is the opening line of the Shema, Deuteronomy 6:4. Wyschogrod does not offer a detailed grammatical or syntactical defense of this argument, probably because his thesis does not rise or fall on this point. His argument is, neverthe-

---

[11] Moshe Weinfeld, *Deuteronomy 1–11: A New Translation with Introduction and Commentary,* The Anchor Bible, vol. 5 (New York: Doubleday, 1991), 328.

[12] See n. 77 for more details on this point.

[13] Weinfeld, *Deuteronomy 1–11,* 328. According to Weinfeld, Deut. 6:12–15 contains the most overt references to the Decalogue.

[14] Ibid.

[15] Ibid.

[16] Wyschogrod, "The 'Shema Israel' in Judaism," 23–24.

less, rooted in the logic of the narrative itself: he asserts that the message of this entire section of text, culminating in the Shema, "is one of concern."[17]

Within Wyschogrod's larger unit (5:1–6:9), I find three smaller units of text preceding the Shema: a historical recital recalling the Sinai covenant and the Decalogue (5:1–21), a narrative explaining how the people of Israel fearfully sent Moses to receive the commands from God on their behalf (5:22–33), and a brief exhortation in which Moses emphasizes the importance of obedience to God's commands (6:1–3).

According to Wyschogrod, Moses' impetus for this elaborate speech (5:1–6:9) is his fear that the people of Israel will neglect the commands of YHWH. What if the people of Israel—who received God's words indirectly through Moses rather than directly from God—begin to doubt the necessity of exclusive devotion and obedience to God? Wyschogrod explains, "The danger Moses foresees is that [the Jewish people] will not serve God with all their hearts. They will not simply forget God. Too much has happened between God and [God's] people to make that likely. The danger is that the God who revealed [God's self] at Sinai will not be their only God."[18]

In an effort to prevent this catastrophe, Moses first reminds Israel of the covenant God made with them, and of how God saved them from slavery; second, of the Decalogue itself; third, that Moses received God's words on behalf of the people at their own insistence, because of their fear; and fourth, of the necessity of faithful obedience. Viewed in this light, the Shema can be seen as the goal of the series of narratives, commands, and exhortations leading up to it: the call to serve God alone, and to love God with one's whole being. The rationale for obeying the Shema is found in Israel's story of faith—the story Moses recalls for Israel.

Weinfeld and Wyschogrod have offered important observations about the Shema's larger literary context—Weinfeld's is based on structural observations, and Wyschogrod's is based on narrative logic. In the next section, I will offer another perspective on the larger literary context of the Shema, incorporating both structure and narrative logic, and drawing on the work of these two scholars.

---

[17] Ibid., 24.

[18] Ibid.

A NEW APPROACH TO THE LITERARY CONTEXT OF THE SHEMA

I propose a literary framework for the Shema beginning at 5:1 with Moses "calling unto" (וַיִּקְרָא אֶל; my translation) the people, and ending at 6:25 with the proclamation, "If we diligently observe this entire commandment before the LORD our God, as he has commanded us, we will be in the right." Wyschogrod is correct in his claim that the Shema is intrinsically connected with the material that precedes it; indeed, the Shema stands as the culmination of the preceding verses. But Weinfeld is also correct in noticing the Shema's connection to the verses that follow, for the Shema serves as the first half of a literary frame for the homily that immediately follows it. While both scholars are essentially correct in their observations about the Shema's larger literary context, neither presents a comprehensive view. Only by considering their claims together—by analyzing the Shema in light of the material both before and after it—can the truest picture of the Shema's literary context be painted. Let us, then, explore this larger literary framework piece by piece, noticing the patterns and structures that will eventually help us understand the radical claims of the Shema.

Section 1: A covenant reminder

The first section of the Shema's larger setting is formed by verses 1–5 of Deuteronomy.

וַיִּקְרָא מֹשֶׁה אֶל־כָּל־יִשְׂרָאֵל	5:1	Moses convened all Israel,
וַיֹּאמֶר אֲלֵהֶם		and said to them
שְׁמַע יִשְׂרָאֵל		Hear, O Israel,
אֶת־הַחֻקִּים וְאֶת־הַמִּשְׁפָּטִים		the statutes and ordinances
אֲשֶׁר אָנֹכִי דֹּבֵר בְּאָזְנֵיכֶ הַיּוֹם		that I am addressing to you today;
וּלְמַדְתֶּם אֹתָם וּשְׁמַרְתֶּם לַעֲשֹׂתָם:		you shall learn them and keep [them] by doing [them].[19]

---

[19] The last two lines are my translation; the rest is from the NRSV. The NRSV translates "you shall learn them and observe them diligently." For an explanation of my translation, see my comments on the significance of the infinitive construct on pages 40–42. (In this case, לַעֲשֹׂתָם is the infinitive construct.) Also, the phrase "keep [them] by doing [them]" functions as an inclusio in this passage, appearing in a similar form in 6:25.

In the first verse, Deuteronomy 5:1, Moses "calls unto" all Israel. His speech begins with a phrase that will soon become familiar: שְׁמַע יִשְׂרָאֵל (Hear, O Israel). This is the first appearance of this phrase in Deuteron- omy but certainly not the last. It will appear twice more in chapter 6 (once in a slightly different form), and once each in chapters 9, 20, and 27. In this first instance, what is Moses calling the people to hear, to obey, to heed? All Israel is called to heed אֶת־הַחֻקִּים וְאֶת־הַמִּשְׁפָּטִים—the "statutes and ordinances" (NRSV) or "laws and rules,"[20] the ones "that I am speaking in your ears today."[21] They are to learn (וּלְמַדְתֶּם) these laws, and to "keep [them] by doing [them]" (וּשְׁמַרְתֶּם לַעֲשֹׂתָם).[22]

יְהוָה אֱלֹהֵינוּ כָּרַת עִמָּנוּ בְּרִית בְּחֹרֵב:	5:2	The LORD our God made a covenant with us at Horeb.
לֹא אֶת־אֲבֹתֵינוּ כָּרַת יְהוָה אֶת־הַבְּרִית הַזֹּאת כִּי אִתָּנוּ אֲנַחְנוּ אֵלֶּה פֹה הַיּוֹם כֻּלָּנוּ חַיִּים:	5:3	Not with our ancestors did the LORD make this covenant, but with us, who are all of us here alive today.
פָּנִים בְּפָנִים דִּבֶּר יְהוָה עִמָּכֶם בָּהָר מִתּוֹךְ הָאֵשׁ:	5:4	The LORD spoke with you face to face at the mountain, out of the fire.
אָנֹכִי עֹמֵד בֵּין־יְהוָה וּבֵינֵיכֶם בָּעֵת הַהִוא לְהַגִּיד לָכֶם אֶת־דְּבַר יְהוָה	5:5	(At that time I was standing between the LORD and you to declare to you the words of the LORD;
כִּי יְרֵאתֶם מִפְּנֵי הָאֵשׁ וְלֹא־עֲלִיתֶם בָּהָר		for you were afraid because of the fire and did not go up the mountain.)

Following verse 1, Moses reminds the people of the covenant at Horeb, emphasizing that this covenant is the one YHWH made with the people of Israel themselves, not with their ancestors (5:3), and by implication, not with Moses their intercessor (5:5). In verses 2–5, YHWH is mentioned by name five times—once as יְהוָה אֱלֹהֵינוּ (YHWH our God), and four

---

[20] Tigay, *Deuteronomy*, 61.

[21] My translation.

[22] My translation.

times as יְהוָה (Yhwh). Additionally, these verses contain two phrases beginning with לֹא, a small word that will soon increase in significance.

Section 2: The Decalogue

The second section of this passage, beginning with the last Hebrew word of Deuteronomy 5:5, is the Decalogue.

לֵאמֹֽר		And he said:
אָֽנֹכִי֙ יְהוָ֣ה אֱלֹהֶ֔יךָ אֲשֶׁ֧ר הוֹצֵאתִ֛יךָ מֵאֶ֥רֶץ מִצְרַ֖יִם	5:6	I am the LORD your God, who brought you out of the land of Egypt,
מִבֵּ֥ית עֲבָדִֽים׃		out of the house of slavery;
לֹֽא־יִהְיֶ֥ה לְךָ֛ אֱלֹהִ֥ים אֲחֵרִ֖ים עַל־פָּנָֽיַ׃	5:7	you shall have no other gods before me.
לֹֽא־תַעֲשֶׂ֨ה־לְךָ֥ פֶ֣סֶל כָּל־תְּמוּנָ֗ה אֲשֶׁ֤ר בַּשָּׁמַ֙יִם֙ מִמַּ֔עַל וַאֲשֶׁ֥ר בָּאָ֖רֶץ מִתָּ֑חַת	5:8	You shall not make for yourself an idol, whether in the form of anything that is in heaven above, or that is on the earth beneath,
וַאֲשֶׁ֥ר בַּמַּ֖יִם מִתַּ֥חַת לָאָֽרֶץ׃		or that is in the water under the earth.
לֹֽא־תִשְׁתַּחֲוֶ֥ה לָהֶ֖ם וְלֹ֣א תָעָבְדֵ֑ם כִּ֣י אָֽנֹכִ֞י יְהוָ֤ה אֱלֹהֶ֙יךָ֙ אֵ֣ל קַנָּ֔א פֹּ֠קֵד עֲוֺ֨ן אָב֧וֹת עַל־בָּנִ֛ים	5:9	You shall not bow down to them or worship them; for I the LORD your God am a jealous God, punishing children for the iniquity of parents,
וְעַל־שִׁלֵּשִׁ֥ים וְעַל־רִבֵּעִ֖ים לְשֹׂנְאָֽי׃		to the third and fourth generation of those who reject me,
וְעֹ֤שֶׂה חֶ֙סֶד֙ לַאֲלָפִ֔ים לְאֹהֲבַ֖י וּלְשֹׁמְרֵ֥י מִצְוֺתֽוֹ	5:10	but showing steadfast love to the thousandth generation of those who love me and keep my commandments.
לֹ֥א תִשָּׂ֛א אֶת־שֵֽׁם־יְהוָ֥ה אֱלֹהֶ֖יךָ לַשָּׁ֑וְא כִּ֣י לֹ֤א יְנַקֶּה֙ יְהוָ֔ה אֵ֛ת אֲשֶׁר־יִשָּׂ֥א אֶת־שְׁמ֖וֹ לַשָּֽׁוְא	5:11	You shall not make wrongful use of the name of the LORD your God, for the LORD will not acquit anyone who misuses his name.

שָׁמֹ֛ור אֶת־יֹ֥ום הַשַּׁבָּ֖ת
לְקַדְּשֹׁ֑ו כַּאֲשֶׁ֥ר צִוְּךָ֖ ׀ יְהוָ֥ה
אֱלֹהֶֽיךָ׃

5:12 Observe the sabbath day and keep it holy, as the LORD your God commanded you.

שֵׁ֤שֶׁת יָמִים֙ תַּֽעֲבֹ֔ד
וְעָשִׂ֖יתָ כָּֽל־מְלַאכְתֶּֽךָ׃

5:13 Six days you shall labor and do all your work.

וְיֹ֙ום֙ הַשְּׁבִיעִ֔י שַׁבָּ֖ת ׀ לַיהוָ֣ה
אֱלֹהֶ֑יךָ
לֹ֣א תַעֲשֶׂ֣ה כָל־מְלָאכָ֡ה

5:14 But the seventh day is a sabbath to the LORD your God; you shall not do any work—

אַתָּ֣ה ׀ וּבִנְךָֽ־וּבִתֶּ֣ךָ
וְעַבְדְּךָֽ־וַֽאֲמָתֶ֡ךָ
וְשֹׁורְךָ֩ וַחֲמֹ֨רְךָ֜ וְכָל־בְּהֶמְתֶּ֗ךָ

you, or your son or your daughter, or your male or female slave, or your ox or your donkey, or any of your livestock,

וְגֵֽרְךָ֙ אֲשֶׁ֣ר בִּשְׁעָרֶ֔יךָ
לְמַ֗עַן יָנ֛וּחַ עַבְדְּךָ֥ וַאֲמָתְךָ֖
כָּמֹֽוךָ׃

or the resident alien in your towns, so that your male and female slave may rest as well as you.

וְזָכַרְתָּ֗ כִּ֣י־עֶ֤בֶד הָיִ֙יתָ֙
בְּאֶ֣רֶץ מִצְרַ֔יִם
וַיֹּצִ֙אֲךָ֜ יְהוָ֤ה אֱלֹהֶ֙יךָ֙ מִשָּׁ֔ם
בְּיָ֥ד חֲזָקָ֖ה וּבִזְרֹ֣עַ נְטוּיָ֑ה

5:15 Remember that you were a slave in the land of Egypt, and the LORD your God brought you out from there with a mighty hand and an outstretched arm;

עַל־כֵּ֗ן צִוְּךָ֙ יְהוָ֣ה אֱלֹהֶ֔יךָ
לַעֲשֹׂ֖ות אֶת־יֹ֥ום הַשַּׁבָּֽת׃

therefore the LORD your God commanded you to keep the sabbath day.

כַּבֵּ֣ד אֶת־אָבִ֗יךָ וְאֶת־אִמֶּ֔ךָ
כַּאֲשֶׁ֥ר צִוְּךָ֖ יְהוָ֣ה אֱלֹהֶ֑יךָ

5:16 Honor your father and your mother, as the LORD your God commanded you,

לְמַ֣עַן ׀ יַאֲרִיכֻ֣ן יָמֶ֗יךָ
וּלְמַ֙עַן֙ יִ֣יטַב לָ֔ךְ עַ֚ל הָֽאֲדָמָ֔ה

so that your days may be long and that it may go well with you in the land

אֲשֶׁר־יְהוָ֥ה אֱלֹהֶ֖יךָ נֹתֵ֥ן לָֽךְ׃

that the LORD your God is giving you.

לֹ֥א תִּרְצָֽח׃

5:17 You shall not murder.

וְלֹ֥א תִּנְאָֽף׃

5:18 Neither shall you commit adultery.

וְלֹא תִּגְנֹב׃ 5:19 Neither shall you steal.

וְלֹא־תַעֲנֶה בְרֵעֲךָ עֵד שָׁוְא׃ 5:20 Neither shall you bear false witness against your neighbor.

וְלֹא תַחְמֹד אֵשֶׁת רֵעֶךָ 5:21 Neither shall you desire your
וְלֹא תִתְאַוֶּה בֵּית רֵעֶךָ neighbor's house, or field, or
שָׂדֵהוּ וְעַבְדּוֹ וַאֲמָתוֹ male or female slave, or ox, or
שׁוֹרוֹ וַחֲמֹרוֹ donkey, or anything that
וְכֹל אֲשֶׁר לְרֵעֶךָ׃ belongs to your neighbor.

The first word that appears in this section, לֵאמֹר (saying), serves as a strong link between the first and second sections—so strong, in fact, that it could arguably be included in the first section, rather than here. This word, לֵאמֹר, presents the Decalogue as an extension of that section's call to "Hear, O Israel." In fact, the words of the Decalogue are presented as the very words YHWH proclaimed to the people at Mount Horeb, under circumstances vividly recounted by Moses in Deuteronomy 5:1–5.

Although the intricacies of the Decalogue are beyond the scope of this study, several of its literary features are pertinent to the questions at hand. In this section, YHWH is mentioned by name exactly ten times—a striking number, echoing the subject matter of this section, and (more subtly) the fact that YHWH's name was mentioned half as many times in the previous section. Of these ten references to YHWH, the first three are to יְהֹוָה אֱלֹהֶיךָ (YHWH your God), the fourth is simply to יְהֹוָה, and the final six are once again to יְהֹוָה אֱלֹהֶיךָ.

The tiny negative לֹא *is used 13 times in this section. The* first six uses of the term occur in verses 6–11, and the final six occur in verses 17–21. Between these two sets of prohibitions rest verses 12–16, the commands to honor the sabbath and one's parents; in the middle of these five verses, we find one more occurrence of לֹא.

Along with the final six references to "YHWH your God," the following events and themes also appear in verses 12–16: slavery in the land of Egypt (בְּאֶרֶץ מִצְרַיִם) in verse 15; that which YHWH commands (צִוְּךָ יְהֹוָה אֱלֹהֶיךָ) in verses 15–16; and the land (הָאֲדָמָה) YHWH is giving to Israel, in verse 16. Although the topic and terminology of land recurs throughout Deuteronomy 5–6, only in verse 16 is it referred to as אֲדָמָה,

rather than אֶרֶץ.[23] Slavery in Egypt is mentioned three times in this passage, twice at the very beginning of the section, in verse 6, and once in verse 15. Yhwh's commands are invoked in verse 10, with obedience to those commands strongly linked with loving Yhwh. It is written that Yhwh will offer steadfast love (חֶסֶד) to those who love (לְאֹהֲבַי) Yhwh and to those who keep the commands (וּלְשֹׁמְרֵי מִצְוֹתוֹ) of Yhwh. Later, we will explore the nature of this link; right now, it is enough to acknowledge that it is there, embedded in the Decalogue, the quintessential list of Yhwh's commands that Israel is expected to keep.

Section 3a: The delegation of Moses

The third section is the one immediately prior to the Shema proper; we will explore it in two smaller segments. The first of these is Deuteronomy 5:22–27.

אֶת־הַדְּבָרִים הָאֵלֶּה דִּבֶּר יְהוָה אֶל־כָּל־קְהַלְכֶם בָּהָר מִתּוֹךְ הָאֵשׁ הֶעָנָן וְהָעֲרָפֶל קוֹל גָּדוֹל	5:22	These words the Lord spoke with a loud voice to your whole assembly at the mountain, out of the fire, the cloud, and the thick darkness,
וְלֹא יָסָף		and he added no more.
וַיִּכְתְּבֵם עַל־שְׁנֵי לֻחֹת אֲבָנִים וַיִּתְּנֵם אֵלָי׃		He wrote them on two stone tablets, and gave them to me.
וַיְהִי כְּשָׁמְעֲכֶם אֶת־הַקּוֹל מִתּוֹךְ הַחֹשֶׁךְ וְהָהָר בֹּעֵר בָּאֵשׁ וַתִּקְרְבוּן אֵלַי כָּל־רָאשֵׁי שִׁבְטֵיכֶם וְזִקְנֵיכֶם׃	5:23	When you heard the voice out of the darkness, while the mountain was burning with fire, you approached me, all the heads of your tribes and your elders;
וַתֹּאמְרוּ הֵן הֶרְאָנוּ יְהוָה אֱלֹהֵינוּ אֶת־כְּבֹדוֹ וְאֶת־גָּדְלוֹ	5:24	and you said, "Look, the Lord our God has shown us his glory and greatness,
וְאֶת־קֹלוֹ שָׁמַעְנוּ מִתּוֹךְ [A]		and we have heard his voice

---

[23] The term אֲדָמָה is used once more in Deuteronomy 5–6, but in that case (Deut. 6:15), it refers to the earth as a whole rather than to Israel's own land: "The anger of the Lord your God would be kindled against you and he would destroy you from the face of the earth."

הָאֵשׁ הַיּ֥וֹם הַזֶּ֖ה רָאִ֑ינוּ
כִּֽי־יְדַבֵּ֧ר אֱלֹהִ֛ים אֶת־הָֽאָדָ֖ם

out of the fire. Today we have seen that God may speak to someone

וָחָֽי׃

and the person may still live.

וְעַתָּה֙ לָ֣מָּה נָמ֔וּת
כִּ֣י תֹֽאכְלֵ֔נוּ הָאֵ֥שׁ הַגְּדֹלָ֖ה
הַזֹּ֑את

5:25 So now why should we die? For this great fire will consume us;

אִם־יֹסְפִ֣ים ׀ אֲנַ֗חְנוּ לִשְׁמֹ֙עַ
אֶת־ק֨וֹל יְהוָ֧ה אֱלֹהֵ֛ינוּ ע֖וֹד

[B] if we hear the voice of the LORD our God any longer,

וָמָֽתְנוּ׃

we shall die.

כִּ֣י מִ֣י כָל־בָּשָׂ֡ר
אֲשֶׁ֣ר שָׁמַ֣ע קוֹל֩ אֱלֹהִ֨ים חַיִּ֜ים
מְדַבֵּ֧ר מִתּֽוֹךְ־הָאֵ֛שׁ כָּמֹ֖נוּ

5:26 [C] For who is there of all flesh that has heard the voice of the living God speaking out of fire, as we have,

וַיֶּֽחִי׃

and remained alive?

קְרַ֤ב אַתָּה֙ וּֽשֲׁמָ֔ע אֵ֛ת כָּל־אֲשֶׁ֥ר
יֹאמַ֖ר יְהוָ֣ה אֱלֹהֵ֑ינוּ

5:27 Go near, you yourself, and hear all that the LORD our God will say.

וְאַ֣תְּ ׀ תְּדַבֵּ֣ר אֵלֵ֗ינוּ אֵת֩ כָּל־
אֲשֶׁ֨ר יְדַבֵּ֜ר יְהוָ֧ה אֱלֹהֵ֛ינוּ
אֵלֶ֑יךָ

Then tell us everything that the LORD our God tells you,

וְשָׁמַ֖עְנוּ
וְעָשִֽׂינוּ׃

and we will hear, and we will do.[24]

Section 3a recounts the situation surrounding the giving of the Decalogue, narrating how the people themselves, out of fear of the life-threatening smoke and fire surrounding YHWH's voice and YHWH's mountain, sent Moses to receive the covenant on their behalf. In these six verses, the name of YHWH is invoked five times, once as יְהוָֹה, then four times as יְהוָה אֱלֹהֵינוּ (YHWH our God). Verse 26 contains a reference to the "living God" (אֱלֹהִים חַיִּים) rather than a reference to YHWH.

In verses 24–26, repetitions of the words אֵשׁ, קוֹל, אֱלֹהִים, יְהוָה, and שְׁמַע *form a striking pattern. In these 3 verses the* (קוֹל) *of voice ?* of

---

[24] The final two clauses are my translation; the NRSV reads, "and we will listen and do it." The rest of the translation is from the NRSV.

YHWH is mentioned twice, while the voice of the "living God" is mentioned once. Each time the voice of YHWH or God is mentioned, the fire (אֵשׁ) associated with YHWH is also mentioned, and also the act of hearing/heeding (שָׁמַע) God's voice. Clustered in this way, these terms create a poignant threefold repetition (see A, B, and C in the text layout above). Following the first group, in verse 24, the people proclaim, "Today we have seen that God may speak to someone and the person may still live וָחָי)." After the second group, in verse 25, the people proclaim that if they continue hearing the voice of YHWH, "we shall die (וָמָתְנוּ)!" Following the third group, in verse 26, the people question: "For who is there of all flesh that has heard the voice of the living God speaking out of fire, as we have, and remained alive (וַיֶּחִי)?"

In the two verses preceding these three groupings (22–23), אֵשׁ and יְהוָה are the only words from this set that have already been employed; in the verse following these three groupings (5:27), שָׁמַע and יְהוָה are the only words from the set that continue to be employed. In this way, the text takes the reader on a journey that begins with the fire of God, which provokes questions about life and death, and which leaves us, in the end, with the conviction that what is constant is יְהוָה and what is required is שָׁמַע—the act of hearing, of listening, and of obedience. Indeed, as we go on, we will discover that this text's most striking literary feature is the fact that varieties of שָׁמַע appear no less than five times. In 5:24, 5:25, and 5:26, it is the voice of YHWH or God that the Israelites will hear (and thus, obey); in 5:27, it is the things YHWH says that the people will hear (and thus, obey). Indeed, the connection between hearing and obedience is emphasized by this text's final two words, which link hearing with doing: וְשָׁמַעְנוּ וְעָשִׂינוּ ("and we will hear, and we will do").[25]

Section 3b: YHWH's acceptance of Moses as delegate

The frequent use of שָׁמַע will continue in the next ten verses.

וַיִּשְׁמַע יְהוָה אֶת־קוֹל	5:28	The LORD heard your words
דִּבְרֵיכֶם בְּדַבֶּרְכֶם אֵלָי		when you spoke to me, and
וַיֹּאמֶר יְהוָה אֵלַי		the LORD said to me:
שָׁמַעְתִּי אֶת־קוֹל דִּבְרֵי		"I have heard the words of

---

[25] My translation.

הָעָם הַזֶּה		this people,
אֲשֶׁר דִּבְּרוּ אֵלֶיךָ הֵיטִיבוּ כָּל־אֲשֶׁר דִּבֵּרוּ׃		which they have spoken to you; they are right in all that they have spoken.
מִי־יִתֵּן וְהָיָה לְבָבָם זֶה לָהֶם לְיִרְאָה אֹתִי	5:29	If only they had such a mind as this, to fear me
וְלִשְׁמֹר אֶת־כָּל־מִצְוֹתַי כָּל־הַיָּמִים לְמַעַן יִיטַב לָהֶם וְלִבְנֵיהֶם לְעֹלָם׃		and to keep all my commandments always, so that it might go well with them and with their children forever!
לֵךְ אֱמֹר לָהֶם שׁוּבוּ לָכֶם לְאָהֳלֵיכֶם׃	5:30	Go say to them, 'Return to your tents.'
וְאַתָּה פֹּה עֲמֹד עִמָּדִי וַאֲדַבְּרָה אֵלֶיךָ אֵת כָּל־הַמִּצְוָה וְהַחֻקִּים וְהַמִּשְׁפָּטִים אֲשֶׁר תְּלַמְּדֵם	5:31	But you, stand here by me, and I will tell you all the commandments, the statutes and the ordinances, that you shall teach them,
וְעָשׂוּ בָאָרֶץ אֲשֶׁר אָנֹכִי נֹתֵן לָהֶם לְרִשְׁתָּהּ׃		so that they may do them in the land that I am giving them to possess."
וּשְׁמַרְתֶּם לַעֲשׂוֹת כַּאֲשֶׁר צִוָּה יְהוָה אֱלֹהֵיכֶם אֶתְכֶם	5:32	You must therefore be careful to do as the LORD your God has commanded you;
לֹא תָסֻרוּ יָמִין וּשְׂמֹאל׃		you shall not turn to the right or to the left.
בְּכָל־הַדֶּרֶךְ אֲשֶׁר צִוָּה יְהוָה אֱלֹהֵיכֶם אֶתְכֶם תֵּלֵכוּ	5:33	You must follow exactly the path that the LORD your God has commanded you,
לְמַעַן תִּחְיוּן וְטוֹב לָכֶם וְהַאֲרַכְתֶּם יָמִים בָּאָרֶץ אֲשֶׁר תִּירָשׁוּן׃		so that you may live, and that it may go well with you, and that you may live long in the land that you are to possess.
וְזֹאת הַמִּצְוָה הַחֻקִּים וְהַמִּשְׁפָּטִים אֲשֶׁר צִוָּה יְהוָה אֱלֹהֵיכֶם	6:1	Now this is the commandment—the statutes and the ordinances—that the LORD your God charged me

לְלַמֵּד אֶתְכֶם		to teach you to observe in the land that you are about to cross into and occupy,
לַעֲשׂוֹת בָּאָרֶץ אֲשֶׁר אַתֶּם		
עֹבְרִים שָׁמָּה לְרִשְׁתָּהּ׃		
לְמַעַן תִּירָא אֶת־יְהוָה	6:2	so that you and your children and your children's children may fear the LORD your God all the days of your life, and keep all his decrees and his commandments that I am commanding you, so that your days may be long.
אֱלֹהֶיךָ לִשְׁמֹר אֶת־כָּל־		
חֻקֹּתָיו וּמִצְוֹתָיו אֲשֶׁר אָנֹכִי		
מְצַוֶּךָ אַתָּה וּבִנְךָ וּבֶן־בִּנְךָ		
כֹּל יְמֵי חַיֶּיךָ וּלְמַעַן		
יַאֲרִכֻן יָמֶיךָ׃		
וְשָׁמַעְתָּ יִשְׂרָאֵל	6:3	Hear therefore, O Israel, and observe them diligently, so that it may go well with you,
וְשָׁמַרְתָּ לַעֲשׂוֹת		
אֲשֶׁר יִיטַב לְךָ		
וַאֲשֶׁר תִּרְבּוּן מְאֹד		and so that you may multiply greatly in a land flowing with milk and honey, as the LORD, the God of your ancestors, has promised you.
כַּאֲשֶׁר דִּבֶּר יְהוָה אֱלֹהֵי		
אֲבֹתֶיךָ לָךְ אֶרֶץ זָבַת חָלָב		
וּדְבָשׁ׃		

In this section of the text, the word שְׁמַע is employed at both the beginning and the end—twice in 5:28, and once in 6:3 as וְשָׁמַעְתָּ יִשְׂרָאֵל. Also mentioned in both 5:28 and 6:3 is YHWH's name—again, it appears twice as a simple יְהֹוָה in verse 28, while in verse 3 it is presented once as the more elaborate יְהוָה אֱלֹהֵי אֲבֹתֶיךָ, translated as "YHWH, God of your ancestors."

Inside this loosely knit frame of references to שְׁמַע and יְהֹוָה, two short passages are contained; the first is a speech of YHWH which Moses is asked to deliver to the people of Israel (5:28–31). In this speech, YHWH ironically commends the Israelites for their fear, a fear that resulted in their sending Moses to receive the commands on their behalf. Jeffrey Tigay speculates that perhaps YHWH compliments the people out of "hope that this reverence will remain with them and motivate them to observe the commandments."[26] If the people would fear God, observing "all of his commandments always" (אֶת־כָּל־מִצְוֹתַי כָּל־הַיָּמִים; v. 29), then it would go well not only for them (יִיטַב לָהֶם) but for their children

---

[26] Tigay, *Deuteronomy*, 73.

(וְלִבְנֵיהֶם). In verse 31, God promises to tell Moses each command (כָּל־הַמִּצְוָה), all the statutes (וְהַחֻקִּים) and ordinances (וְהַמִּשְׁפָּטִים), so that Moses may teach them to the people, and so that the people may practice them in the land (בָאָרֶץ) that God is giving them. The first chunk of text, then, records YHWH's reaction to the people's fear, in addition to YHWH's promise to convey the commands to the people through Moses.

The second short passage (5:32–6:3) presents a series of exhortations about these commands. Three times Israel is advised to do all that YHWH their God has commanded them (צִוָּה יְהוָה אֱלֹהֵיכֶם); three times are God's commands themselves invoked (varieties of מִצְוָה); once each YHWH's "statutes and ordinances" and "all his decrees" are mentioned (6:1 and 6:2, respectively).

Both passages contain references to the land (5:31; 5:33; 6:1; 6:3); both contain claims that following the commands of YHWH will cause it to "go well with" the people of Israel (5:29; 5:33; 6:3). In fact, it could be argued that at the heart of this text is verse 5:33, a verse that ties together all but one of the major themes of this section:

בְּכָל־הַדֶּרֶךְ אֲשֶׁר צִוָּה יְהוָה אֱלֹהֵיכֶם אֶתְכֶם תֵּלֵכוּ	5:33	You must follow exactly the path that the LORD your God has commanded you,
לְמַעַן תִּחְיוּן וְטוֹב לָכֶם וְהַאֲרַכְתֶּם יָמִים בָּאָרֶץ אֲשֶׁר תִּירָשׁוּן׃		so that you may live, and that it may go well with you, and that you may live long in the land that you are to possess.

The commands of YHWH, the wish that "it may go well with you," and living in the land—these themes are repeated over and over in Deuteronomy 5–6. These are the themes that flow in and around and through the claims of the Shema. In fact, it is only the theme of שָׁמַע itself—the theme of hearing, listening, and obeying—that is not found explicitly in 5:33. However, שָׁמַע is the very theme that unites section 3a (5:22–27) with section 3b (5:28–6:3). In 5:22–27, שָׁמַע is used five times; in 5:28–6:3, שָׁמַע is used three times (once together with יִשְׂרָאֵל). In this way, the very first שָׁמַע in 5:1 is joined by eight others in 5:28–6:3.

Section 4: The Shema

Together, these nine uses of the word שָׁמַע prepare the way for 6:4, the beginning of the Shema itself, in which שָׁמַע is used for its tenth and final time.

שְׁמַע יִשְׂרָאֵל יְהוָה אֱלֹהֵינוּ יְהוָה אֶחָד׃	6:4	Hear, O Israel: The LORD is our God, the LORD alone.
וְאָהַבְתָּ אֵת יְהוָה אֱלֹהֶיךָ בְּכָל־לְבָבְךָ וּבְכָל־נַפְשְׁךָ וּבְכָל־מְאֹדֶךָ׃	6:5	You shall love the LORD your God with all your heart, and with all your soul, and with all your might.
וְהָיוּ הַדְּבָרִים הָאֵלֶּה אֲשֶׁר אָנֹכִי מְצַוְּךָ הַיּוֹם עַל־לְבָבֶךָ׃	6:6	Keep these words that I am commanding you today in your heart.
וְשִׁנַּנְתָּם לְבָנֶיךָ וְדִבַּרְתָּ בָּם בְּשִׁבְתְּךָ בְּבֵיתֶךָ וּבְלֶכְתְּךָ בַדֶּרֶךְ	6:7	Recite them to your children and talk about them when you are at home and when you are away,
וּבְשָׁכְבְּךָ וּבְקוּמֶךָ׃		when you lie down and when you rise.
וּקְשַׁרְתָּם לְאוֹת עַל־יָדֶךָ וְהָיוּ לְטֹטָפֹת בֵּין עֵינֶיךָ׃	6:8	Bind them as a sign on your hand, fix them as an emblem on your forehead,
וּכְתַבְתָּם עַל־מְזוּזֹת בֵּיתֶךָ וּבִשְׁעָרֶיךָ׃	6:9	and write them on the doorposts of your house and on your gates.

Within the Shema's first three clauses are a cluster of four terms that are now familiar to us: שְׁמַע יִשְׂרָאֵל (Hear, O Israel!); יְהוָה אֱלֹהֵינוּ (YHWH our God); יְהוָה אֱלֹהֶיךָ (YHWH your God); יְהוָה and (YHWH). We have already discussed how שְׁמַע יִשְׂרָאֵל functions as a linguistic key in this text, serving to prepare the reader for the profound declaration that is the Shema. Because the word שָׁמַע is used eight times in the text connecting the Decalogue to the Shema, we can be relatively certain, first, that the reader is meant to make a profound connection between these two seminal texts. Second, the fact that the word שָׁמַע occurs ten times in the text as a whole serves as a second, numerical connection to the Decalogue: just as there are ten "words," so are there ten uses of

שְׁמַע. It is appropriate, then, that the tenth and final שְׁמַע is the most significant, the one in which the most meaning is concentrated, the one in which YHWH's enigmatic name appears three times in the first nine words. In fact, it is YHWH's name that functions as the second linguistic key in the Shema's larger literary context, a phenomenon that we will explore in a moment.

The remainder of the Shema is remarkable—unique—in the context of these two chapters, and in the book of Deuteronomy thus far. There are only a few familiar words in verses 5–9: we hear about the words YHWH commands (מְצַוְּךָ) in verse 7; we hear about instructing the children (לְבָנֶיךָ) about YHWH's words/commands—a theme that will sound familiar as we approach the end of chapter 6. However, much of what these four verses claim is new. We hear of loving YHWH for the first time in Deuteronomy—a theme recurrent as Deuteronomy unfolds, but brand new here. Additionally, we are instructed to "talk about" the words YHWH commands at all times, and to fashion concrete reminders about these words, reminders that will adorn both our bodies and our residences. This material recurs in Deuteronomy 11; indeed, in the canon as a whole, it resonates with Exodus 13. But at this point in Deuteronomy, it is distinctive.

Section 5: Israel's story retold

I have argued that Deuteronomy 5:23–6:3 serves to link the Decalogue and the Shema not only practically but also linguistically. Additionally, I believe that 6:10–19 is linked to both the Decalogue and the Shema. The most obvious link to the Decalogue is the appearance of a multitude of לֹא (not) phrases.

וְהָיָה כִּי יְבִיאֲךָ יְהוָה אֱלֹהֶיךָ אֶל־הָאָרֶץ	6:10	When the LORD your God has brought you into the land
אֲשֶׁר נִשְׁבַּע לַאֲבֹתֶיךָ לְאַבְרָהָם לְיִצְחָק וּלְיַעֲקֹב לָתֶת לָךְ		that he swore to your ancestors, to Abraham, to Isaac, and to Jacob, to give you
עָרִים גְּדֹלֹת וְטֹבֹת אֲשֶׁר לֹא־בָנִיתָ		—a land with fine, large cities that you did not build,
וּבָתִּים מְלֵאִים כָּל־טוּב אֲשֶׁר לֹא־מִלֵּאתָ וּבֹרֹת חֲצוּבִים	6:11	houses filled with all sorts of goods that you did not fill, hewn cisterns

אֲשֶׁר לֹא־חָצַ֫בְתָּ

that you did not hew,

כְּרָמִים וְזֵיתִים
אֲשֶׁר לֹא־נָטַעְתָּ
וְאָכַלְתָּ וְשָׂבָעְתָּ׃

vineyards and olive groves that you did not plant— and when you have eaten your fill,

הִשָּׁ֫מֶר לְךָ֫ פֶּן־תִּשְׁכַּח אֶת־יְהֹוָה

6:12   take care that you do not forget the LORD,

אֲשֶׁר הוֹצִיאֲךָ֫ מֵאֶ֫רֶץ מִצְרַ֫יִם מִבֵּית עֲבָדִים׃

who brought you out of the land of Egypt, out of the house of slavery.

אֶת־יְהֹוָה אֱלֹהֶ֫יךָ תִּירָא וְאֹתוֹ תַעֲבֹד וּבִשְׁמוֹ תִּשָּׁבֵעַ׃

6:13   The LORD your God you shall fear; him you shall serve, and by his name alone you shall swear.

לֹא תֵלְכוּן אַחֲרֵי אֱלֹהִים אֲחֵרִים מֵאֱלֹהֵי הָעַמִּים אֲשֶׁר סְבִיבוֹתֵיכֶם׃

6:14   Do not follow other gods, any of the gods of the peoples who are all around you,

כִּי אֵל קַנָּא יְהֹוָה אֱלֹהֶ֫יךָ בְּקִרְבֶּ֫ךָ

6:15   because the LORD your God, who is present with you, is a jealous God.

פֶּן־יֶחֱרֶה אַף־יְהֹוָה אֱלֹהֶ֫יךָ בָּךְ וְהִשְׁמִידְךָ֫ מֵעַל פְּנֵי הָאֲדָמָה׃

The anger of the LORD your God would be kindled against you and he would destroy you from the face of the earth.

לֹא תְנַסּוּ אֶת־יְהֹוָה אֱלֹהֵיכֶם כַּאֲשֶׁר נִסִּיתֶם בַּמַּסָּה׃

6:16   Do not put the LORD your God to the test, as you tested him at Massah.

שָׁמוֹר תִּשְׁמְרוּן אֶת־מִצְוֹת יְהֹוָה אֱלֹהֵיכֶם וְעֵדֹתָיו וְחֻקָּיו אֲשֶׁר צִוָּךְ׃

6:17   You must diligently keep the commandments of the LORD your God, and his decrees, and his statutes that he has commanded you.

וְעָשִׂ֫יתָ הַיָּשָׁר וְהַטּוֹב בְּעֵינֵי יְהֹוָה לְמַ֫עַן יִיטַב לָךְ

6:18   Do what is right and good in the sight of the LORD, so that it may go well with you,

וּבָאתָ וְיָרַשְׁתָּ אֶת־הָאָ֫רֶץ

and so that you may go in and

הַטֹּבָה אֲשֶׁר־נִשְׁבַּע יְהוָה
לַאֲבֹתֶיךָ:

occupy the good land that the
LORD swore to your ancestors
to give you,

לַהֲדֹף אֶת־כָּל־אֹיְבֶיךָ   6:19
מִפָּנֶיךָ כַּאֲשֶׁר דִּבֶּר יְהוָה:

thrusting out all your enemies
from before you, as the LORD
has promised.

There are six לֹא phrases in this passage, nearly half the number (thirteen) that appear in the Decalogue itself. However, of the six לֹא
phrases in this pericope, only the last two serve as prohibitions similar
in content to those of the Decalogue. The first four לֹא phrases, appearing in verses 10–11, designate acts that Israel did not perform, as follows: "When the LORD your God has brought you into the land that he
swore to your ancestors, to Abraham, to Isaac, and to Jacob, to give
you—a land with fine, large cities that you did *not* build, houses filled
with all sorts of goods that you did *not* fill, hewn cisterns that you did
not hew, vineyards and olive groves that you did *not* plant."[27]

These verses describe the covenant faithfulness of YHWH, the one
who brought Israel into the land promised to its people. These לֹא
phrases thus emphasize the magnanimous nature of YHWH's deliver-
ance. Israel was the recipient of cities and homes and food and drink
for which they did not labor; all these things were given to them by
God's initiative. The last two לֹא phrases appear in verse 14, "Do *not*
follow other gods, any of the gods of the peoples who are all around
you," and in verse 16, "Do *not* put the LORD your God to the test, as you
tested him at Massah."

Verse 14 is a clear referent to what Christians designate the first of
the Ten Commandments, and to what Jews designate the second of the
ten words: "You shall have no other gods before me" (Deut. 5:7). Verse
16 does not have a clear parallel in the Decalogue; however, it is obvi-
ously connected to the history of Israel's wilderness wanderings, specifically to Exodus 17, when the people of Israel complained of thirst in
the wilderness. In response to their cry, YHWH instructed Moses to
strike a rock, from which water would pour forth. The people's thirst
was quenched; however, every time this incident is mentioned in scripture, it is mentioned in a negative light. In every biblical text mention-

---

[27] My italics.

ing Massah, it is written that the people "tested" God, and this "testing" is considered evidence of weakness and failure. These texts (which include Deuteronomy 9:22, Deuteronomy 33:8, and Psalm 95:8–9) express the idea that to test God is to doubt God's faithfulness, perhaps even to doubt God's sovereignty. In this way, then, perhaps verse 16 is by implication also related to the first command of the Decalogue.

The last two לֹא phrases, then, arguably serve to connect this pericope with the Decalogue. But so do its many references to YHWH. Verses 10–19 mention the name of YHWH ten times, a striking number, especially considering that (1) the name of YHWH was invoked ten times in the course of the Decalogue, and (2) since 5:1, the word שָׁמַע has also been invoked ten times. Of the ten references to YHWH, four refer to YHWH "your [sing.] God," two refer to YHWH "your [pl.] God," and four refer only to YHWH. One final literary feature connects this pericope to the Decalogue. In 6:15, after the לֹא phrase prohibiting the worship of other gods, YHWH is called "a jealous God" (כִּי אֵל קַנָּא יְהוָה אֱלֹהֶיךָ). A similar declaration in 5:9 is found in the midst of the commandment forbidding idol worship (כִּי אָנֹכִי יְהוָה אֱלֹהֶיךָ אֵל קַנָּא).

Other familiar phrases in this pericope include a reference to the land of Egypt and the house of slavery (v. 12); two references to the land YHWH has promised Israel (vv. 10, 18); and references to YHWH's commands, orders, statutes, and decrees (v. 17).

We have explored the way this pericope relates to the Decalogue. How it relates to the Shema will become clear as we examine our final bit of text.

Section 6: The teaching for children

This final pericope can be divided into two sections, the first consisting of verse 20 alone.

	6:20	
כִּי־יִשְׁאָלְךָ בִנְךָ מָחָר לֵאמֹר מָה הָעֵדֹת וְהַחֻקִּים וְהַמִּשְׁפָּטִים		When your children ask you in time to come, "What is the meaning of the decrees and the statutes and the ordinances
אֲשֶׁר צִוָּה יְהוָה אֱלֹהֵינוּ אֶתְכֶם:		that the LORD our God has commanded you?"

This verse presents the question that Israel's children will inevitably ask. In the Masoretic Text (MT), the first part of their question is much

Errata

Take this Word to Heart: The Shema in Torah and Gospel

page 21, paragraph 3:
The tiny negative לֹא is used thirteen times in this section. The first six uses of the term occur in verses 6–11, and the final six occur in verses 17–21. Between these two sets of prohibitions rest verses 12–16, the commands to honor the sabbath and one's parents; in the middle of these five verses, we find one more occurrence of לֹא.

page 23, last paragraph:
In verses 24–26, repetitions of the words אֵשׁ,קוֹל,אֱלֹהִים,יְהוָה, and שָׁמַע form a striking pattern. In these three verses, the voice (קוֹל) of

page 28, bottom of page:
Within the Shema's first three clauses are a cluster of four terms that are now familiar to us: שְׁמַע יִשְׂרָאֵל (Hear, O Israel!); יְהוָה אֱלֹהֵינוּ (YHWH our God); יְהוָה אֱלֹהֶיךָ (YHWH your God);and יְהוָה (YHWH). We

page 49, n. 77
[1] Weinfeld believes there are four ways to solve the semantic puzzle of Deut. 6:4: (1) YHWH is our God, YHWH is one; (2) YHWH is our God, YHWH alone; (3) YHWH our God is one YHWH; or (4) YHWH our God, YHWH is one. Weinfeld argues that in Deuteronomy, the words יְהוָה and אֱלֹהֵינוּ never occur as subject and predicate; rather, אֱלֹהֵינוּ always

simpler than the NRSV's translation above: "What *are* the decrees and the statutes and the ordinances . . . ?"[28]

The second section prescribes the appropriate reply to this query, a reply grounded concretely in the story of Israel.

6:21 then you shall say to your children, "We were Pharaoh's slaves in Egypt, but the LORD brought us out of Egypt with a mighty hand.

וְאָמַרְתָּ לְבִנְךָ
עֲבָדִים הָיִינוּ לְפַרְעֹה
בְּמִצְרָיִם וַיּוֹצִיאֵנוּ יְהֹוָה
מִמִּצְרַיִם בְּיָד חֲזָקָה׃

6:22 The LORD displayed before our eyes great and awesome signs and wonders against Egypt, against Pharaoh and all his household.

וַיִּתֵּן יְהֹוָה אוֹתֹת וּמֹפְתִים
גְּדֹלִים וְרָעִים בְּמִצְרַיִם
בְּפַרְעֹה וּבְכָל־בֵּיתוֹ לְעֵינֵינוּ׃

6:23 He brought us out from there in order to bring us in, to give us the land that he promised on oath to our ancestors.

וְאוֹתָנוּ הוֹצִיא מִשָּׁם לְמַעַן
הָבִיא אֹתָנוּ לָתֶת לָנוּ
אֶת־הָאָרֶץ אֲשֶׁר נִשְׁבַּע
לַאֲבֹתֵינוּ׃

6:24 Then the LORD commanded us to observe all these statutes, to fear the LORD our God,

וַיְצַוֵּנוּ יְהֹוָה לַעֲשׂוֹת אֶת־
כָּל־הַחֻקִּים הָאֵלֶּה לְיִרְאָה
אֶת־יְהֹוָה אֱלֹהֵינוּ

for our lasting good, so as to keep us alive, as is now the case.

לְטוֹב לָנוּ כָּל־הַיָּמִים לְחַיֹּתֵנוּ
כְּהַיּוֹם הַזֶּה׃

6:25 If we diligently observe this entire commandment before the LORD our God, as he has commanded us, we will be in the right."[29]

וּצְדָקָה תִּהְיֶה־לָּנוּ
כִּי־נִשְׁמֹר לַעֲשׂוֹת אֶת־כָּל־
הַמִּצְוָה הַזֹּאת לִפְנֵי
יְהֹוָה אֱלֹהֵינוּ כַּאֲשֶׁר צִוָּנוּ׃

Verses 21 and 22 refer to the people's slavery in Egypt; verse 23 reminds the children that YHWH delivered them from slavery "in order to

---

[28] My translation of the MT.

[29] As in 5:1 (see n. 19), the Hebrew phrase which the NRSV translates above as "if we diligently observe" could also be translated as "if we keep [this entire commandment] by doing [it]."

... give us the land that he promised on oath to our ancestors"; verses 24 and 25 shift to focus on the commandments and statutes themselves, and their consequences "for our lasting good," "to keep us alive," and so that "we will be in the right."

This answer seems a strange response to the children's question. To the simple question, "What are the commandments?" a more natural response would be to quote the Decalogue or the Shema. Why offer an account of Israel's history as an answer, especially an account in which, apart from "fearing the LORD," no commandment is named? Perhaps an examination of the way this pericope links to what has come before will help as we consider these questions.

This section's focus on the instruction of children makes an obvious connection to the Shema—a connection so strong and clear that Weinfeld understands this pericope, along with the Shema, as framing the homily in 6:10–19. These final six verses depict what it means to recite the words of YHWH to one's children, as commanded in the Shema.

Moreover, this pericope shares important vocabulary with the first verses of chapter 5. In both 5:1 and in 6:20, the phrase "statutes and ordinances" (וְהַחֻקִּים וְהַמִּשְׁפָּטִים) occurs, while slightly different versions of the phrase "to keep [the laws] by doing [them]" occur in 5:1 and in 6:25.[30] Although "laws and rules" appears once in the Decalogue, this longer phrase "to keep [the laws] by doing [them]" occurs only at the beginning of chapter 5 and at the end of chapter 6. An inclusio is formed by the recurrence of these terms, implying that the material that lies between them is linked. This inclusio also underscores the unity of Deuteronomy 5–6, a unity within which the Decalogue and the Shema are both explicitly and implicitly connected. Thus, the answer to the children's query in 6:20–25 is layered with meaning. Small reminders of both the Decalogue and the Shema, which (it can be argued) together sum up the whole Torah, are embedded in the historical recital and exhortations that make up this pericope. Indeed, the mysterious unity of God's words is such that the whole of God's statutes, decrees, and ordinances can be denoted, in the singular, "the command"—as is done in both 6:1 and 6:25, forming yet another inclusio uniting chapter 6.

---

[30] נִשְׁמֹר לַעֲשׂוֹת in 5:1, וּשְׁמַרְתֶּם לַעֲשֹׂתָם in 6:20.

THE DECALOGUE AND THE SHEMA IN DEUTERONOMY 5–6

Before moving on, it may be helpful to revisit, clarify, and sum up a few of the many ways connections between the Decalogue and the Shema are made in Deuteronomy 5–6.

Repetitions of the name of יְהוָה link the Decalogue and the Shema with their surrounding literary context. The numbers themselves are telling: in section one (recalling the covenant), YHWH is used five times; in section two (the Decalogue), YHWH is used ten times; in sections three (the section connectiong Decalogue to Shema), YHWH is used twelve times; in section four (the Shema itself), YHWH is used three times; in section five (Israel's story retold), YHWH is again used ten times; and in section six (the teaching for children), YHWH is used six times. Although the correlations between form and content are not perfect here, the numbers are certainly striking. Both the sheer quantity of references to YHWH and the near symmetry of those references (5-10-12; 3-10-6)[31] are impressive, causing one to acknowledge the skilled hand(s) that, in all likelihood, purposefully and carefully wove these texts together.

Furthermore, the literary connections among the six sections of Deuteronomy 5–6 are many and complex. Section two is connected to section five by the many לֹא phrases in each and by their common references to slavery in Egypt and the land promised by God. Section two is connected to section three because of the parallels in subject matter (section two is the Decalogue; section three narrates the giving of the Decalogue), not to mention the fact that the ten words (or commandments) of section two are suggestive of the ten *shemas* that will soon accumulate, eight of which occur in section three. These *shemas* in turn connect section three to the Shema itself (section four), while the Shema itself is connected to section six by the concern the texts share for the education of children. And section six's references to commands and land connect it with sections two and five, while an inclusio also links it to section one.

---

[31] If the sections I have designated three and four were combined (as Deut. 5:22–6:9)—which would be possible because the tenth and final שְׁמַע of section four acts as the culmination of the nine previous uses of שְׁמַע, eight of which fall in section three—then the symmetry would be even stronger: 5-10-15-10-6.

Also, as Jeff Williams has discovered, broad parallels are easily found in Deuteronomy 5–6. Williams writes:

> Starting in Deuteronomy 5, we see the order of the call to Israel (Hear, O Israel—v. 1), the teaching of the central ethical principle (the Decalogue—vv. 6–21), a short homily on obedience as a requirement for prosperity (vv. 22–33), and an exhortation on teaching children the principle (6:1–3). Starting in Deuteronomy 6:4–25 we see a similar structure: the call to Israel (Hear, O Israel (v. 4), the teaching of the central ethical principle (vv. 4–5), a short homily on obedience (vv. 10–19), and an exhortation on teaching children (vv. 20–25).[32]

Here, Williams points out that the Decalogue and the Shema are presented as two parallel ethical principles in Deuteronomy 5–6. Because of this parallelism, Williams argues that readers of Deuteronomy are "expected to associate the Decalogue with the Shema, understanding them as roughly similar, perhaps even as equivalent."[33]

For all these reasons, and for others cited earlier, I believe Deuteronomy 5–6 functions as a literary unit, a unit that purposefully connects the Decalogue to the Shema, and vice versa. The implication is that obedience to God's commands (embodied in the Decalogue) and loving God (embodied in the Shema) are actions intricately bound up with one another—as intricately bound up as are the Shema and the Decalogue in these two chapters of Deuteronomy. In the following sections, we will test this thesis by exploring aspects of the Shema in its larger Deuteronomic context, as well as in its historical/liturgical contexts.

The Shema: Deuteronomic perspectives

In order to explore the Shema in its larger Deuteronomic context, I will examine the recurrences of two of its most important features in the context of Deuteronomy as a whole: first, the notable phrase שְׁמַע יִשְׂרָאֵל; and second, the concept that humans are commissioned to love (אהב) YHWH.

---

[32] See chapter three in this book, Jeff T. Williams, "The Significance of Love of God and Love of Neighbor in Luke's Gospel," 87, n. 43.

[33] Ibid., 87.

In the Hebrew Bible, the construction "Hear, O Israel" is found only in Deuteronomy. Specifically, the phrase is found in six places, three of which we have already examined (Deut. 5:1, 6:3, and 6:4). The other three instances occur in Deuteronomy 9:1, 20:3, and 27:9. For the sake of comparison, we will examine each in turn. First, in Deuteronomy 9:1, the NRSV reads: "Hear, O Israel! You are about to cross the Jordan today, to go in and dispossess nations larger and mightier than you, great cities, fortified to the heavens." This proclamation begins a new section of text—a new Mosaic sermon, if you will. In this chapter and the next,

> Moses continues to address dangers to faith that might develop
> as a consequence of the conquest, a theme he began in chapters
> 7 and 8. Here he preaches against the feeling of self-righteous-
> ness that defeating the Canaanites might engender. He states
> that victory can be no proof of virtue, for Israel's history has
> been one of continuous provocation and rebellion. . . . Moses
> concludes by calling on Israel not to act rebelliously in the future
> but to serve God and obey [God's] commands.[34]

Thus, in chapter 9, שְׁמַע יִשְׂרָאֵל precedes an exhortation that the Israelites are to live humbly in the land of promise, never forgetting the God who made a way for them, never forgetting their obligation of obedience to this God. Indeed, a significant portion of chapter 9 is devoted to yet another retelling of the giving of the Decalogue (vv. 8–21), this time with an emphasis on Israel's disregard for God's commands.[35]

Second, in Deuteronomy 20:2–4, the NRSV reads: "Before you engage in battle, the priest shall come forward and speak to the troops, and shall say to them: 'Hear, O Israel! Today you are drawing near to do battle against your enemies. Do not lose heart, or be afraid, or panic, or be in dread of them; for it is the LORD your God who goes with you, to fight for you against your enemies, to give you victory.'"

---

[34] Tigay, *Deuteronomy*, 96.

[35] See, for example, vv. 23–24: "And when the LORD sent you from Kadesh-barnea, saying, 'Go up and occupy the land that I have given you,' you rebelled against the command of the LORD your God, neither trusting him nor obeying him. You have been rebellious against the LORD as long as he has known you."

In this passage, as in the first, the people of Israel are reminded that, because YHWH is with them, they need not fear their enemies, not even when they are at war and must face "horses and chariots, an army larger than [their] own" [20:1]. In chapter 20, the laws of warfare are included in Deuteronomy's larger presentation of all the laws of the land, a presentation that begins in 11:31 and does not end until 26:15.[36] Third, in Deuteronomy 27:9–10, the NRSV reads: "Then Moses and the levitical priests spoke to all Israel, saying: Keep silence and hear, O Israel! This very day you have become the people of the LORD your God. Therefore obey the LORD your God, observing his commandments and his statutes that I am commanding you today."[37] These two verses function as an "appeal for obedience"[38] in the midst of a chapter outlining a reaffirmation of Israel's covenant with YHWH, a reaffirmation marking Israel's arrival in the land.

An examination of the contexts of these three additional occurrences of שְׁמַע יִשְׂרָאֵל makes it obvious that each is inextricably linked with the concept of obedience to YHWH's commands. Chapter 9 begins with the שְׁמַע phrase, continues with another narrative of the Decalogue, and ends with an exhortation for obedience. Chapter 20 is a part of the Deuteronomic retelling of the law itself—in this case, the שְׁמַע phrase is concretely embedded within the commands of YHWH that are to be obeyed. Deuteronomy 27:9–10 offers connections to obedience that are both obvious and subtle: first, the שְׁמַע phrase is closely followed by an explicit command to obey; second, these two verses are wedged into a larger text mandating a liturgy of covenant renewal, which implicitly recalls the Sinai covenant and the giving of the law itself.[39]

---

[36] Tigay, *Deuteronomy*, 117.

[37] Tigay remarks: "This is the first time that the appeal to hear is preceded by a call for silence. Absolute concentration is required at the awesome moment when Israel becomes the people of God and in order for everyone to be prepared for the solemn promises and warnings they are about to hear" (ibid., 251).

[38] Ibid., 250.

[39] Deuteronomy's first "Hear, O Israel" phrase and its final "Hear, O Israel" phrase explicitly mention the observance of YHWH's commands. The first occurrence is in Deut. 5:1: "Moses convened all Israel, and said to them: Hear, O Israel, the statutes and ordinances that I am addressing to you today; you shall learn them and observe them diligently." This verse bears a notable similarity to Deut. 27:9–10, which contains the final

We have established, then, that each time שְׁמַע יִשְׂרָאֵל is used in Deuteronomy, exhortations for obedience can be found nearby. Next, by examining Deuteronomic conceptions of loving God, we will also discover the intimate Deuteronomic relationship between the act of loving YHWH and the act of obeying YHWH's commands.

Of the twenty-two verses in Deuteronomy containing אהב, twelve address human love for God;[40] of those twelve, an overwhelming nine explicitly connect love with obedience;[41] of those nine, five connect love with obedience in such a way that their exact relationship is ambiguous,[42] while four make the connection between love and obedience clear.[43] For example, Deuteronomy 11:1 ambiguously states: "You shall love the LORD your God, therefore, and keep his charge, his decrees, his ordinances, and his commandments always." In both the English and the Hebrew texts,[44] the construction of this sentence leaves one unsure whether loving God and keeping God's commandments are the same action or two separate (yet equally mandated) actions. The same ambiguity exists in the following verse: "Choose life so that you and your descendants may live, loving the LORD your God, obeying him, and holding fast to him; for that means life to you and length of days, so that you may live in the land that the LORD swore to give to your ancestors, to Abraham, to Isaac, and to Jacob" (Deut. 30:19b–20).[45]

שְׁמַע phrase: "Then Moses and the levitical priests spoke to all Israel, saying: Keep silence and hear, O Israel! This very day you have become the people of the LORD your God. Therefore obey the LORD your God, observing his commandments and his statutes that I am commanding you today."

[40] These are Deut. 5:10; 6:5; 7:9; 10:12; 11:1; 11:13; 11:22; 13:3; 19:9; 30:6; 30:16; and 30:19b–20.

[41] These include all those listed above except Deut. 6:5; 13:3; and 30:6. The other nine all include references to obeying/keeping/doing the commandments, obeying God's voice, or walking in God's ways.

[42] These five are 5:10; 7:9; 10:12–13; 11:1; and 30:19b–20.

[43] These four are 11:13; 11:22; 19:9; 30:16.

[44] In the Hebrew, this verse is even more ambiguous than in the English. First, both וְאָהַבְתָּ (love) and וְשָׁמַרְתָּ (keep) are finite verbs that stand alone, related to one another only in the most uncertain manner. Also, in the Masoretic Text, the word *therefore* is not present in this verse. Thus, it is impossible to juggle the word order and read this verse as saying: "You shall love the Lord your God, and *therefore* keep his commandments."

[45] In the previous example (see n. 44), ambiguity was created because *both* "love" and

However, there remain four verses in Deuteronomy in which love and obedience are connected much more clearly. Unfortunately, this clarity is expressed in only two of the NRSV translations, as follows:

> [YHWH] will give you all the land that he promised your ancestors to give you, provided you diligently observe this entire commandment that I command you today, by loving the LORD your God and walking always in his ways—then you shall add three more cities to these three. (Deut. 19:8b–9)

> If you obey the commandments of the LORD your God that I am commanding you today, by loving the LORD your God, walking in his ways, and observing his commandments, decrees, and ordinances, then you shall live and become numerous, and the LORD your God will bless you in the land that you are entering to possess. (Deut. 30:16)

In these two cases, one little word—"by"—makes all the difference. According to these verses, one obeys God's commands *by* loving God and walking in God's ways (in the second instance, also *by* observing God's commandments, decrees, and ordinances). In this way, loving God and obeying God's commands become synonymous—one is fulfilled by the doing of the other. One might wonder if the inclusion of the word "by" in these verses is warranted; I believe it is. In both cases, "to love" is presented as an infinitive construct, לְאַהֲבָה.[46] In biblical He-

---

"keep" are finite verbs; this time, ambiguity is created because *neither* "love" nor "obey" is finite. In this verse, both verbs are infinitives construct. Because of their status as infinitives, the relationship of these verbs to the finite verb "choose" is clear (choose life by loving and obeying); however, their relationship to each other is still cloudy. This is also the case in Deut. 10:12–13: "So now, O Israel, what does the LORD your God require of you? Only to fear the LORD your God, to walk in all his ways, to love him, to serve the LORD your God with all your heart and with all your soul, and to keep the commandments of the LORD your God and his decrees that I am commanding you today, for your own well-being." Ambiguity also exists in Deut. 5:10 ("but showing steadfast love to the thousandth generation of those who love me and keep my commandments") and Deut. 7:9 ("Know therefore that the LORD your God is God, the faithful God who maintains covenant loyalty with those who love him and keep his commandments, to a thousand generations"). In both cases, "love" and "keep" are participles; once again, clarity is elusive because neither is a finite verb.

[46] I am indebted to Perry Yoder for offering insight into the importance of the infinitive construct here.

brew, the infinitive construct form of a verb "almost always occurs in relation to another verb."[47] In fact, "semantically speaking, the infinitive has no function in itself. The functions of an infinitive refer either to the syntactic function that it fulfils in a clause, or to the semantic relationship between itself and the finite verb."[48] In other words, in the first example above (Deut. 19:8b–9), the infinitive construct לְאַהֲבָה could not function apart from its relationship to the finite verb תִּשְׁמֹר (to watch, observe, obey). For this reason, "by loving" is an accurate translation, although "to love" would also be acceptable. The second example (Deut. 30:16) is more complex. In the Masoretic Text (MT), the first clause of this verse is omitted, so that it begins as follows:

אֲשֶׁר אָנֹכִי מְצַוְּךָ הַיּוֹם ... that I am commanding you today,
לְאַהֲבָה אֶת־יְהוָה אֱלֹהֶיךָ by loving the LORD your God ...[49]

This puzzling text leaves us with an infinitive construct (לְאַהֲבָה) with no finite verb nearby; the verbal form מְצַוְּךָ is a participle. To resolve this problem, Tigay renders אֲשֶׁר as "for" and מְצַוְּךָ as finite, thus translating this verse as follows: "For I command you this day, to love the LORD your God, to walk in His ways, and to keep His commandments."[50] If we follow the MT as Tigay does, then this text no longer provides clarity about the relationship between love and obedience. We could instead base our translation on the LXX, as the NRSV seems to do:

ἐὰν εἰσακούσῃς   If you obey
τὰς ἐντολὰς   the commandments
κυρίου τοῦ θεοῦ σου   of the LORD your God
ἃς ἐγὼ ἐντέλλομαί σοι   that I am commanding you
σήμερον   today,
ἀγαπᾶν κύριον   by loving the LORD
τὸν θεόν σου   your God ...[51]

[47] Christo H. J. van der Merwe, Jackie A. Naude, and Jan H. Kroeze, *A Biblical Hebrew Reference Grammar* (Sheffield, England: Sheffield Academic Press, 2000), 153.

[48] Ibid., 155.

[49] My translation.

[50] Tigay, *Deuteronomy*, 287.

[51] NRSV.

If we follow the LXX, the first clause is much less puzzling, and the relationship between obedience and love is clarified: ἀγαπᾶν (love) is an infinitive which depends on the finite verb εἰσακούσῃς (hear, obey) for its meaning; once again, we obey by loving. Even if this option is rejected, however, the clarity of the former text (Deut. 19:8b–9) still stands, and it is supported by two more verses which in the MT clearly express the relationship between love and obedience, even if they do not do so in the NRSV, as quoted below:

> If you will only heed his every commandment that I am commanding you today—loving the LORD your God, and serving him with all your heart and with all your soul—then he will give the rain for your land in its season. (Deut. 11:13–14a)

> If you will diligently observe this entire commandment that I am commanding you, loving the LORD your God, walking in all his ways, and holding fast to him, then the LORD will drive out all these nations before you. (Deut. 11:22–23)

These translations again exhibit ambiguity. However, in both cases, the form of the Hebrew verb "to love" is once again a qal infinitive construct, while the form of the verb "to heed/observe" is finite. Thus, there is no reason not to insert the word "by" in these verses:

> If you will only heed his every commandment that I am commanding you today—by loving the LORD your God, and serving him with all your heart and with all your soul . . .

> If you will diligently observe this entire commandment that I am commanding you, by loving the LORD your God, walking in all his ways, and holding fast to him . . .

As a result, we can be confident in claiming that three (and arguably four) of the nine verses in Deuteronomy that explicitly connect love to obedience do so in a way that makes it difficult to distinguish acts of love for God from acts of obedience to God's commands.[52] In fact, in

---

[52] It is also interesting to note the other two places in Deuteronomy where Israel is commanded to love God with all their heart and soul: "You must not heed the words of those prophets or those who divine by dreams; for the LORD your God is testing you, to know whether you indeed love the LORD your God with all your heart and soul" (Deut. 13:3, NRSV); "Moreover, the LORD your God will circumcise your heart and the heart of

these verses, loving YHWH is presented as one way a person can live in obedience to YHWH's commands; one can obey YHWH by loving YHWH, or even more strongly, obeying YHWH is equivalent to loving YHWH. Thus, our brief investigation into the occurrences in the larger Deuteronomic context of שְׁמַע יִשְׂרָאֵל and אָהַב—two key words in the Shema proper—have both brought us face to face with the commands of YHWH and our imperative to obey them.

THE SHEMA: HISTORICAL AND LITURGICAL PERSPECTIVES

If we consider for a moment the way the Shema has been analyzed over the centuries, we will discover that the connection we have been exploring between love and obedience is supported not only by the larger context of Deuteronomy but also by several key developments in the history of the Shema's interpretation. First, we will revisit the popular modern theory that the Shema is based on ancient Near Eastern suzerain-vassal treaties; second, we will explore the rabbinic teaching that the recitation of the Shema is an act of "accepting the yoke of the kingdom of God"; third, we will turn to the Qumran community and the Dead Sea Scrolls to see what they might teach us about liturgical practices and the Shema in the early centuries CE.

With other contemporary scholars,[53] Herman Horowitz argues that an accurate reading of the Shema is rooted in the suzerain-vassal treaties of the ancient Near East, treaties that scholars believe were in use before and during the time the Deuteronomic writings were being produced and edited.[54] These treaties held the following structural elements in common:

1) a declaration and introduction describing the historical reasons for the treaty—usually the prior benevolence of the su-

---

your descendants, so that you will love the LORD your God with all your heart and with all your soul, in order that you may live" (Deut. 30:6, NRSV).

[53] This theory is so widely supported that it is nearly impossible to present a comprehensive list of scholars who subscribe to it. However, two (in addition to Horowitz) who support this theory are Moshe Weinfeld and Carolyn Pressler. See Weinfeld, *Deuteronomy 1–11*, 354 and Carolyn Pressler, "The Shema: A Protestant Feminist Reading," in *Escaping Eden: New Feminist Perspectives on the Bible,* ed. Harold C. Washington, Susan Lochrie Graham, and Pamela Thimmes (Sheffield, England: Sheffield Academic Press, 1998), 47–48.

[54] Herman L. Horowitz, "The Sh'ma Reconsidered," *Judaism* 24 (Fall 1975): 476–81.

zerain or Great King toward his vassal, in return for which undivided loyalty is expected;

2) a series of stipulations which govern the deeds of the parties who have established the treaty relationship between them;

3) the identification of the Great King, either in [the king's] own name or through a third party who imposes an oath on the vassal in behalf of the king;

4) the invocation of a threat or curse against the party to the treaty who breaches the agreement;

5) the names of the witnesses to the treaty; and

6) provisions for a periodic recital of the treaty.[55]

Horowitz argues that all of these structural elements are present in the three passages traditionally associated with the Shema in Jewish liturgy: Deuteronomy 6:4–9, Deuteronomy 11:13–21, and Numbers 15:37–41. He explains the connections in this way: Deuteronomy 6:4 reveals to the people of Israel "the Great King to whom it must direct its undivided loyalty," thus fulfilling the first and third requirements;[56] Deuteronomy 6:5–9 offers stipulations for achieving the afore-mentioned loyalty, thus fulfilling the second requirement; Deuteronomy 11:13–17 describes how Israel will be cursed if they do not abide by the covenant, but blessed if they do, thus fulfilling the fourth requirement; Numbers 15:37–41 provides for witnesses to the covenant, thus fulfilling the fifth requirement.[57] Although Horowitz does not mention this element, the Shema's provisions for morning and evening recitation provide opportunity for the fulfillment of the sixth requirement.

Of most interest for this essay is the fact that, within suzerain-vassal treaties, the vassals often agreed to "love" their suzerains. This love was interpreted as loyalty, and loyalty demanded obedience to the treaty's stipulations. If the stipulations were broken, then loyalty (love) was severed, and the treaty was no longer binding. Moshe Weinfeld elaborates on the suzerain-vassal concept of love. "Love with all the heart means sole recognition of the beloved to the exclusion of any rival," Weinfeld states. "Indeed, 'love' in the ancient Near East connotes

---

[55] Horowitz, "The Sh'ma Reconsidered," 476.

[56] Ibid., 477.

[57] Ibid.

loyalty. Thus, when the suzerain demands loyalty from his vassal, he adjures him that he shall love the king as he loves himself."[58] In essence, a command for such love is a command for "exclusive devotion."[59] Weinfeld also points out that the language of "with all your heart," "with all your soul," and "with all your might" is characteristic of suzerain-vassal treaties. Furthermore, Weinfeld argues that in suzerain-vassal language, "with all the soul" corresponds to the fact that the vassal must be prepared to die for the suzerain, while "with all your might" corresponds to the demand that one appear before the sovereign in the company of all one's military forces. Thus, it is not surprising when one ancient Near Eastern treaty expects the vassal to come "to aid [the suzerain] with full heart ... with your army and your chariots and ... be prepared to die...."[60] How neatly those concepts transfer in rabbinic thought—"with all the soul" demanding martyrdom, as demonstrated by Rabbi Akiba, and "with all thy might" demanding all of one's financial and material resources.[61]

Presenting the Shema as a treaty between God and Israel is suggestive of an interpretation of the Shema that surfaced in the ancient world,[62] one that distinguishes itself as particularly resonant with the theology of the Deuteronomic school,[63] namely: *kabbalat 'ol malkhut*

---

[58] Weinfeld, *Deuteronomy 1-11*, 351.

[59] Ibid.

[60] Ibid.

[61] *b. Ber 61b.*

[62] Although scholars are not sure when this interpretation of the Shema first appeared, it is known that in the Yavnean Age (70–220 CE), the Shema was liturgically revised to include this notion of kingship. Thus, it is reasonable to conclude that "yoke of the kingdom" interpretation became active during the Yavnean Age at the latest, and perhaps before. For more information, see Tzvee Zahavy, "Three Stages in the Development of Early Rabbinic Prayer," in *From Ancient Israel to Modern Judaism: Intellect in Quest of Understanding,* ed. Jacob Neusner, Ernest S. Frerichs, and Nahum M. Sarna (Atlanta: Scholars Press, 1989), 233–65.

[63] In this vein, Horowitz argues that the Shema undergirds the Deuteronomic emphasis on the responsibility of the individual to remain faithful to the covenant "through personal pious deeds." Thus, the Shema was grounded in the new theological idea that, although "God's name dwelt in the Sanctuary" at Jerusalem, God did not dwell in the sanctuary—rather, God dwelt everywhere. By reciting the Shema daily, each Judean was "accepting the yoke of the kingdom of God"—a yoke that emphasized both the responsibility of people to abide by the terms of the covenant and the character of God

shammayim, "the acceptance of the yoke of the kingdom of God."[64] This school of interpretation is associated most closely with Deuteronomy 6:4–9 (as opposed to the other two units of text included in the Shema proper); in this school, verse 4 is interpreted as a blessing of the eternal kingship of YHWH, while the remaining material is focused on the individual's acceptance "of the duty of performing the commandments."[65] In this way, the recital of the Shema is more than simply a confession of faith; it also seeks to effect change on the one reciting it by "establish(ing) and renew(ing), periodically, a powerful and all-pervading bond between Israel and God."[66]

Weinfeld illuminates the power of this interpretation by revealing its possible ancient Near Eastern parallels: "In the rabbinic tradition the Shema testimony was defined as the 'acceptance of the yoke of the kingdom of heaven' which perfectly fits the imagery of loyally serving the sovereign on earth. Thus, for example, Nabonidus, the king of Babylon, says [of himself] that 'by mentioning his honorable name let all his enemies bear his yoke forever.'"[67] And just as Nabonidus insists that his enemies bear his yoke, so does he bear the yoke of the divine, declaring that he "keeps the words of the gods," that he "prays to them with all his heart," and that "his neck is bowed to draw their yoke."[68] Additionally, Weinfeld writes that in Akkadian, the idiom "yoke of the kingdom" is the conventional expression for fulfilling one's duties to the sovereign.[69] In short, the acceptance of the yoke is equivalent to taking a pledge of loyalty. Thus, the ancient "yoke of the kingdom" interpretation of the Shema and the modern suzerain-vassal interpretation of the

---

as a deity centered on faithful love and covenant-keeping, a deity whose presence could not be scattered even if God's people were. Here, any Judean "could now rehearse daily [his or her] fervent loyalty to the covenant with God, thus assuring both [their own] and [their] people's acceptability to their Divine sponsor in history." This covenantal understanding of the Shema is rooted in radical monotheism, "a universal divine kingship awaiting historical actualization" (Horowitz, "The Sh'ma Reconsidered," 478).

[64] Ibid., 476.

[65] *m. Ber.* 2:2; also Tigay, *Deuteronomy*, 440.

[66] Ibid., 480.

[67] Weinfeld, *Deutereonomy 1–11*, 352.

[68] Ibid.

[69] Ibid.

Shema converge in the assertion that loving God is being loyal to God, and loyalty connotes—even demands—obedience.[70]

This connection between love and obedience—and indeed, the more concrete connection between the Shema and the Decalogue—is also corroborated by the findings at Qumran, in which a number of teffilin and mezuzot were discovered.[71] It is no surprise that included in the tefillin/mezuzot are the first two passages of the liturgically defined Shema (Deuteronomy 6:4–9 and Deuteronomy 11:13–21). What is impressive is that seven of the tefillin and one of the mezuzot also "[quote] the Decalogue from Deuteronomy."[72] Esther Eshel analyzes one of these ancient artifacts, 4QDeut[n], and comes to the conclusion that this text was used for liturgical purposes, that in fact, 4QDeut[n] is an example of a collection "of Biblical passages that may have been used as a 'prayer book.'"[73] Eshel continues:

---

[70] According to Weinfeld, the liturgical recitation of the Shema in Second Temple Judaism worked in the following manner: CANTOR: Sh'ma Israel, Adonai Elohaynu; ALL: Adonai Ehad. Then, the rest of the Shema was recited, followed immediately by an affirmation of the Shema proclaimed by the congregation, reminiscent of the fealty oaths sworn to emperors. This oath-like affirmation, called the *Emet weyassib* prayer, contains "a formal affirmation of the demands of God the sovereign . . .; a declaration about taking upon themselves the kingdom of God . . .; a declaration of the validity of the obligation for coming generations . . .; and a declaration about the exclusiveness of divine kingship" (Weinfeld, *Deuteronomy 1–11*, 353–54).

[71] Two types of tefillin were discovered at Qumran. The first contained only the passages later required by rabbinic law: Exod. 13:1–10; Exod. 13:11–16; Deut. 6:4–9 (the Shema itself); and Deut. 11:13–21 (the second passage in the liturgical rendition of the Shema). However, other tefillin contained additional passages (such as the Decalogue). Lawrence Schiffman writes of this phenomenon: "Because the Rabbis forbade insertion of additional passages to those required, scholars have theorized that those tefillin found at Qumran containing only required passages are Pharisaic-type tefillin. The Qumran sectarian tefillin are those which contain additional passages. Although this conclusion seems plausible, we have no way of proving such a contention." See Lawrence Schiffman, *Reclaiming the Dead Sea Scrolls: The History of Judaism, the Background of Christianity, the Lost Library of Qumran* (New York: Doubleday, 1994), 309–311.

[72] Esther Eshel, "4QDeut[n]—A Text That Has Undergone Harmonistic Editing," *Hebrew Union College Annual* 62 (1991), ed. Herbert H. Paper (Cincinnati: Hebrew Union College, 1992), 122.

[73] Eshel, "4QDeut[n]," 151.

The scroll contains the following prayer: the blessing after meals . . . and the Decalogue and the Shema. . . . In the [Qumran community's] Manual of Discipline we find . . . [a text] which proves that a blessing in connection with a meal was part of the Qumranic ceremony. The Decalogue and the Shema were said by the priest during Shaharit (morning prayer) in the Temple, as attested in Mishnah Tamid 5,1. . . . We also know that the custom to say the Decalogue was adopted by the Jewish population in Eretz-Israel. Josephus tells us that the Shema was not said only in the Temple, but twice a day by every Jew. In light of this evidence it might be that 4QDeut[n] . . . [is] a collection of prayers excerpted from Deuteronomy and Exodus.[74]

Also supporting a liturgical connection between the Shema and the Decalogue is the existence of the Nash Papyrus, an ancient fragment on which is inscribed both the Shema and the Decalogue. Scholars believe this papyrus, like 4QDeut[n], was used liturgically in the Second Temple period.[75]

The historical evidence for the connection between the Shema and the Decalogue—between love and obedience—can be summed up with three statements. First, there is ample confirmation that when the Shema was included in the book of Deuteronomy, the language of love for God had overtones of the suzerain-vassal treaty, and thus, loving God connoted loyalty to God and obedience to God's commands. Second, the ancient theological principle that to recite the Shema was to accept the "yoke of the kingdom" is a conviction that values obedience to YHWH's commands as an act of fealty to one's sovereign. Third, there is also evidence from Qumran and from the Nash Papyrus that in the Second Temple period, the Shema and the Decalogue were recited together liturgically, thus proving that—at least at these moments in Jewish history—love for YHWH and obedience to YHWH's commands were together the calling of those who worshiped YHWH.

CONCLUSIONS

At least two conclusions can be drawn from this study of love, obedience, and the Shema. First, I believe that the understanding of the

---

[74] Eshel, "4QDeut[n]," 151–52.

[75] Eshel, "4QDeut[n]," 123.

Shema presented in this essay helps untangle a complex semantic issue in Deuteronomy 6:4. Second, the findings offered here also begin to set the stage for the New Testament idea of the Shema as the great commandment. Additionally, I will offer an answer to the objection[76] that an understanding of the Shema as I have presented it in this essay will result in a faith based on what some Protestant Christians have called "works righteousness"—a faith characterized as stringent, as valuing good deeds more than devotion.

First, let us address the debate introduced earlier in this study: What is the meaning of the word אֶחָד in Deuteronomy 6:4—"one" or "alone"? Scholarly opinion on this issue is varied, with R. W. L. Moberly, Vladimir Orel, J. Gerald Janzen, and Moshe Weinfeld arguing for "one,"[77] while S. Dean McBride argues for "alone."[78] Considering the

---

[76] In naming this objection, I have in mind no one particular scholar, article, or school of thought. Rather, I am responding to a hypothetical objection readers of this essay might voice.

[77] Weinfeld believes there are four ways to solve the semantic puzzle of Deut. 6:4: (1) YHWH is our God, YHWH is one; (2) YHWH is our God, YHWH alone; (3) YHWH our God is one YHWH; or (4) YHWH our God, YHWH is one. Weinfeld argues that in Deuteronomy, the words יְהוָה and אֱלֹהֵינוּ *never occur as subject and predicate,* rather אֱלֹהֵינוּ always stands in apposition to יְהוָה. Thus, the first two options are invalid, according to Weinfeld. He also rejects the final option because of the awkwardness of the discontinued first subject. That leaves Weinfeld with but one viable option, the third. And in the grammatical construction used by the third option, "one" is the only possible translation for *echod*. However, he qualifies his answer by writing: "The connotation of 'one' here is not solely unity but also aloneness." Thus, Weinfeld claims that we should translate אֶחָד as "one," while understanding that it also connotes "alone"! See Weinfeld, *Deuteronomy 1–11*, 337–38. Moberly agrees with Weinfeld. See R. W. L. Moberly, "Toward an Interpretation of the Shema," in *Theological Exegesis: Essays in Honor of Brevard S. Childs,* ed. Christopher R. Seitz; Kathryn Greene-McCreight (Grand Rapids: Eerdmans, 1999): 124–44. Vladimir Orel argues: "If the Shema is understood as a proclamation of faith, it must be structurally re-analyzed so that it may be interpreted as an unambiguous expression of one semantic message." His solution? Following Exod. 34:6, he analyzes the first YHWH as a third masculine singular imperfect of *hwh*, thus translating: "Our God *is* one YHWH." The strength of this interpretation, he says, is that the clause is now one clause with one unambiguous message, and the Shema is a definition of God or God's name. Orel does not defend his decision to translate אֶחָד as "one"—likely he is doing so because "one" is the most frequent gloss on אֶחָד. See Vladimir Orel, "The Words on the Doorpost," *Zeitschrift fur die Alttestamentliche Wissenschaft* 109, no. 4 (1997): 614–17. For an argument that connects אֶחָד with the proclamation of God's moral unity, see J. Gerald Janzen, "The Claim of the Shema," *Encounter* 59 (1998): 243–57; and "On the

Shema's many contexts as explored in this essay, the idea that YHWH *alone* is God makes more sense here than the idea that YHWH is somehow and metaphysically *one*. We have already noticed innumerable links, large and small, between the Shema and the Decalogue, and from these connections we have ascertained that loving YHWH and obeying YHWH's commands are inextricably linked. Because of this link, it makes sense to consider the Decalogue when we interpret the Shema. The first thing forbidden in the Decalogue is the worship of other gods, a command that underlines YHWH's uniqueness, but nowhere in the Decalogue is YHWH's unity described or even alluded to. Thus, the connection between Decalogue and Shema offers a compelling rationale for translating אֶחָד in Deuteronomy 6:4 as "alone" rather than "one."[79]

Most Important Word in the Shema (Deuteronomy 6:4–5)," *Vetus Testamentum* 37, no. 3 (1987): 280–300.

[78] S. Dean McBride ("Yoke of the Kingdom: An Exposition of Deuteronomy 6:4–5," *Interpretation* 27 [July 1973]: 273–306) is an ardent advocate for translating אֶחָד here as "alone." He claims that rabbinic Judaism began to interpret Deuteronomy 6:4 as an affirmation of the unity of God in opposition to both Gnostic and Christian theologies as early as the third century CE. However, McBride argues that the verse was originally read as a confession of God's sovereignty, an oath of allegiance to YHWH alone. Thus, he argues: "The classical Jewish sources reveal two overlapping stages in the interpretation of the opening line of the Shema. In this first, it articulates a radical monotheism, a universal divine kingship awaiting historical actualization. In the second, developed largely in response to Christian theology and persecution, it became a statement of the immutable oneness of the single divine Being" (279). What classical Jewish sources does he quote to support this statement? Only the midrash with which this essay began, and a reference to Zech. 14:9: "And YHWH will become king over the whole earth in that day; YHWH will be *ehad* and his name *ehad*." McBride also cites ancient Ugaritic and Arabic sources which use a cognate of *echod* to mean "alone."

[79] As noted in n. 77, scholars sometimes reject "alone" as a translation for אֶחָד because, in the book of Deuteronomy, the words יְהוָה and אֱלֹהֵינוּ never occur as subject and predicate; rather, אֱלֹהֵינוּ always stands in apposition to יְהוָה. Thus, the most common translation of Deut. 6:4 using "alone" is disqualified because it demands using יְהוָה and אֱלֹהֵינוּ as subject and predicate ("YHWH is our God, YHWH alone"). Although this point is salient, I reject it as an adequate reason for choosing "one" over "alone." Granted, אֶחָד is translated as "one" more often than "alone" in the Hebrew Bible. Granted, "alone" does not fit all possible translations of Deut. 6:4 (for example: YHWH is our God, YHWH is one; YHWH our God is one YHWH; YHWH our God, YHWH is one; see Weinfeld, *Deuteronomy 1–11*, 337–38). However, even if one bears these reservations in mind, it is still possible for אֶחָד to be translated as "alone," because (1) "alone" *is* a linguistically permissible

Second, while the synoptic Gospels clearly connect the Shema with the Levitical command to love one's neighbor, this connection has not been made within any of the Shema's contexts explored in this study, at least not explicitly. The Shema overtly commands love of God, but nowhere in Deuteronomy 4–5 is love of neighbor similarly commanded. However, the connection between Decalogue and Shema established herein does open the door to the connection between love of God and love of neighbor. Many of the prohibitions contained within the Decalogue address our relationship with our neighbor, most explicitly in the commands about adultery, theft, false witness, murder, and coveting. And if one considers the Decalogue as representative of all of the commands in the Torah, this point balloons in significance, because many Torah commandments have to do with maintaining right relationships with other people in one's community. Thus, the connection between Decalogue and Shema offers a foundation on which are based later Jewish and Christian theologies linking love of God to love of neighbor.

Finally, how do we answer the objection that the reading of the Shema I have presented in this essay is nothing more than an endorsement of "works righteousness"? I would begin with the well-known Jewish conviction that the first word of the Decalogue is a word of grace, a word reminding the community that this God whose commands they are to obey, this God whom they are to love with all that is theirs—this is the God who delivered them from Egypt even before they had become God's covenant people. The Exodus as an emblem of God's gracious initiative in history thus serves as the foundation for Israel's life together, including the community's own efforts to live in love for God and in obedience to God's commands. In fact, it is the gracious liberation of Yhwh that inspires such obedience, and that makes Yhwh a God worth obeying. Obedience to Yhwh's commands is not a method for obtaining righteousness; rather, it is an expression of love for the God who has been and continues to be the people's deliverer. Obedience thus functions as both an act of gratitude for the liberation that has already occurred and an act of hope for the liberation that is yet to come.

---

gloss for אֶחָד, and (2) it is also linguistically permissible for יְהוָה and אֱלֹהֵינוּ to occur as subject and predicate. Thus, even on purely linguistic grounds, it is not possible to rule out "alone" altogether. Indeed, as I argue in this essay, I believe the Shema's literary and historical contexts tip the scales firmly in the other direction.

CHAPTER TWO

The Shema in Mark:
For a Gentile or a Jewish audience?

James W. Carlson

A
s is well known, the synoptic Gospels—Matthew, Mark, and Luke—each contain a similar formulation of the double love command in association with Jesus. All three authors cite Deuteronomy 6:5 and Leviticus 19:18 in juxtaposition. But only in Mark's Gospel does Jesus quote the entire Shema, Deuteronomy 6:4–5; no other evangelist has Jesus (or anyone else) quote Deuteronomy 6:4.[1]

Why does Mark include Deuteronomy 6:4? The dominant hypothesis is that Mark quoted the Shema from its beginning in order to assert the oneness of God vis-à-vis the polytheism of the Greco-Roman pantheon. Indeed, many facets in the pericope of Mark 12:28–34 demonstrate the author's intent in communicating the gospel to a Gentile audience. Four major features are usually adduced: the interpretation of the Shema as underscoring God's oneness, the emphasis on the moral as opposed to the cultic law, the use of distinctively Hellenistic vocabulary, and the identity of the scribe as a Greek wisdom figure.

Is a Gentile audience the only plausible explanation for Mark's quotation of the Shema? Could he have quoted it for a Jewish audience? This essay will examine this question of Mark's use of the Shema, Deuteronomy 6:4, with the double love command. First, I will present the dominant hypothesis, which posits a Gentile audience, and I will analyze it point by point. Second, I will reanalyze each point in reverse order, positing a Jewish audience instead. I will give attention espe-

---

[1] In Luke's version (Luke 10:25–28), it is a lawyer who quotes Deut. 6:5 and Lev. 19:18.

cially to comparing the ideas expressed in Mark's pericope with those of other Jewish literature from the Second Temple period.

THE SHEMA IN MARK: QUOTED FOR A GENTILE AUDIENCE?

Deuteronomy 6:4 in Mark

The story of the double love command appears in Mark 12:28–34. One of the scribes, in an unusually affable manner, asks Jesus which commandment is the first in the Torah. Jesus answers with two commandments, quoting Deuteronomy 6:5 and Leviticus 19:18. This combination appears in Matthew and Luke, too, but in the Markan version, Jesus prefaces Deuteronomy 6:5 with the Shema proper, Deuteronomy 6:4: "The first is, 'Hear, O Israel: the Lord our God, the Lord is one" (Mark 12:29).[2]

Much debate surrounds the meaning of the last word in Deuteronomy 6:4: אֶחָד. The word is translated as either "one" or "alone."[3] Did the author intend to stress the singularity of God ("one") or the fact that YHWH was the only God whom Israel should serve ("alone")? In Mark, the emphasis is clearly on the oneness of God, given the scribe's affirmation in 12:32: "You are right, Teacher; you have truly said that 'he is one, and besides him there is no other.'"[4] Thus, Mark's quotation of the Shema and his subsequent monotheistic interpretation of it are taken as evidence of his concern to communicate this truth to a Gentile audience. Pheme Perkins, one proponent of this view, writes: "Mark's version of the story suggests that it had been used as part of the preaching to Gentiles. Look up 1 Thess 1:9f. It is a short formula from Paul's mission of preaching to Gentiles. You will notice that such preaching had to begin (which preaching to Jews did not) with teaching the worship of the one true God."[5]

---

[2] Unless otherwise indicated, quotations of scripture are from the NRSV.

[3] See the discussion by Jackie Wyse in chapter one of this book for an interpretation of the Shema in its Deuteronomic context.

[4] Quoting Deut. 4:35.

[5] Pheme Perkins, *Love Commands in the New Testament* (New York: Paulist Press, 1982), 23.

The law in Mark

The two most important commandments in the Torah, Jesus said, are the ones that command love for God and love for neighbor. He elevates these above all others. Mark quotes Jesus as saying that these twin commandments are the greatest: "There is no other commandment greater than these" (Mark 12:31b). The scribe extends his interpretation and comments: "This is much more important than all whole burnt offerings and sacrifices" (Mark 12:33c).

Compared to burnt offerings and sacrifices, the double love command is περισσότερόν (much more important); the scribe's use of the comparative adds emphasis.[6] He makes a clear distinction about the priority of the Torah commandments: the moral laws are more important than the cultic ones. Jesus does not oppose the scribe's comment about the Torah but in 12:34 commends his insight. Some interpreters understand this emphasis on the moral law over against the cultic law as another feature the Markan community used in their outreach to the Gentiles: the purpose of Jesus' formulation of the double love command was to elucidate the moral emphasis in the Torah. Victor Paul Furnish, another proponent of this view, brings together the two aspects I have discussed so far: "What is emphasized (in Mark), doubtless for apologetic-missionary purposes (to Gentiles), is the necessary connection between belief in the one God and obedience to the moral (as contrasted with the cultic) law."[7]

Hellenistic vocabulary in Mark

A few terms in Mark 12:28–34 stand out as appealing to a Hellenistic-Gentile audience. Foremost, Mark quotes Deuteronomy 6:4–5 and Leviticus 19:18 almost verbatim from the Septuagint (LXX). Mark's rendering is different from the other two Synoptic pericopes, as is most evident in their quotation of Deuteronomy 6:5. Matthew's quotation of Deuteronomy 6:5 is much closer to the original Hebrew. In Matthew 22:37, the author uses the Greek ἐν (in), which corresponds to the He-

---

[6] R. T. France, *The Gospel of Mark: A Commentary on the Greek Text,* New International Greek Testament Commentary (Grand Rapids: Eerdmans, 2002), 481.

[7] Victor Paul Furnish, *The Love Command in the New Testament* (Nashville: Abingdon Press, 1972), 30. See Günther Bornkamm, "Das Doppelgebot der Liebe," in *Geschichte und Glaube,* part 1; *Gesammelte Aufsätze,* vol. 3 (Munich: Chr. Kaiser Verlag, 1968), 27–45.

brew ב (in), in the list of faculties with which we should love God. Matthew lists three faculties, the number given in Deuteronomy 6:5 in the Hebrew Bible. Luke appears to have combined elements from both the Hebrew and the Greek Bible. In Luke 10:27, he uses ἐξ (from) once and ἐν three times in the list of faculties.[8] Mark, however, precedes each faculty with the preposition ἐξ, which corresponds exactly to the LXX.

But Mark adds a faculty to the list found in the Hebrew Bible, one that would appeal to Greeks. The term is διάνοια (mind). The idea of loving God with our minds is borrowed from ancient Greek philosophy. The emphasis on the mind as a human faculty to be used in loving God is further underscored by the scribe's recapitulation of Jesus' quotation in 12:33. The scribe substitutes another term for mind and says, "And 'to love him with all the heart, and with all the *understanding*, and with all the strength' . . . is much more important than all whole burnt offerings and sacrifices." The Greek word used is σύνεσις, which means "understanding, intelligence, insight." Clearly, then, by this reference to the mind, Mark intended to communicate that we use our cerebral abilities in loving God.

Another Greek term appears in Jesus' commendation of the scribe. According to Mark 12:34, "When Jesus saw that he answered *wisely*, he said to him, 'You are not far from the kingdom of God.'" The Greek word used is νουνεχῶς, which is a compound of νοῦς (mind) and ἔχω, from the verb "to have." It means "thoughtfully" or "wisely."[9] This word, a *hapax legomenon* in the New Testament, is attested in Aristotle and other Greek sources.[10] Wisdom was a popular theme among the Greeks in the ancient world.

Taken together, these terminological features seem to present the gospel as a rational message, for purposes of reaching Greek pagans. Victor Paul Furnish summarizes Mark's use of this vocabulary: "These words, plus the good Greek formula employed in verse 32, 'In truth you have said,' and the word 'wisely' in verse 34a (used only here in the

---

[8] For a discussion of the text of the Shema as it appears in Luke, see the discussion by Jeff Williams in chapter three of this book.

[9] νουνεχῶς, in *Greek-English Lexicon of the New Testament and Other Early Christian Literature*, 2nd ed., ed. W. Bauer, W. F. Arndt, F. W. Gingrich, F. W. Danker (Chicago: University of Chicago Press, 1979), 544.

[10] Ibid.

whole New Testament) give the Markan version a decidedly rationalistic aspect."[11]

The scribe in Mark

It should be obvious by now that Mark's scribe in this pericope has contributed a great deal to the hypothesis that Mark is writing for Gentile readers. This scribe responds to Jesus' teaching sympathetically, a response uncharacteristic of the scribes portrayed elsewhere in Mark and in the other two synoptic Gospels. Mark identifies him as "*one of the* scribes" (12:28), perhaps to stress that this particular scribe was not representative of their number. This scribe is not hostile to Jesus but engages in a polite and mutually affirming dialogue with him. Rudolph Bultmann labeled this type of exchange a "scholastic dialogue," in contrast to the "controversy dialogues" in Matthew and Luke.[12] The context of the double love command in Matthew and Luke involves a lawyer (νομικός) who is seeking to test Jesus. The Markan version is much more irenic in tone.

The scribe's commentary on Jesus' two commandments, as we have seen, is interpreted as supporting the Hellenistic-Gentile thesis. The scribe makes it clear that by quoting the Shema, Jesus means to underscore God's oneness (vv. 29–31). He understands the human faculty of the mind as referring to our mortal understanding (vv. 30, 33). The scribe sees the purpose in Jesus' formulation of the double love command as putting emphasis on the moral law over against the cultic law (vv. 29, 30, 33). Because of these factors, some proponents of this view portray him more as a wisdom figure than as a Jewish scribe. Johannes Nissen, for example, writes: "It has been suggested that the story as it was used by Mark represented the scribe as a seeker after wisdom (as in Wis 6.17–20). He comes to Jesus, the mediator of wisdom, and leaves with a new understanding of the law gained from that wisdom. In this way the story explains how Christians can worship the true God and stand in the Old Testament tradition without continuing to follow the ritual and cultic obligations of the law."[13]

---

[11] Furnish, *The Love Command*, 29.

[12] Rudolf Bultmann, *The History of the Synoptic Tradition* (Oxford: Blackwell, 1963), 54–55.

[13] Johannes Nissen, "The Distinctive Character of the New Testament Love Command in Relation to Hellenistic Judaism," in *The New Testament and Hellenistic Judaism,* ed. Peder

The foregoing material defines the standard scholarly interpretation regarding Mark's use of the Shema: he quoted it for a Gentile audience. Furthermore, the entire Mark 12:28–34 pericope was formulated to appeal to a Gentile audience. Victor Paul Furnish, the foremost proponent of this view, summarizes the cumulative weight of the evidence:

> The overall point is just this: What is important for true religion is belief in and the worship of the true God and obedience to the moral law, not religious ceremony or cultic performance. When the distinctively rationalistic vocabulary here is coupled with the emphasis upon the oneness of God, the result is material which would have particular merit and meaning within the context of Hellenistic-Jewish and Christian apologetic, directed against Greek polytheism. Moreover, when the double love commandment to love God and the neighbor is specifically set over against the cultic requirements of "whole burnt offerings and sacrifices" another typically anti-pagan motif emerges.[14]

THE SHEMA IN MARK: QUOTED FOR A JEWISH AUDIENCE?

Is there another way to interpret Mark's use of the Shema? Are there other explanations for the presence in Mark's pericope of the themes noted above? I will seek to answer these questions by comparing these themes with those of Jewish literature of Mark's contemporaries, especially the literature of the Second Temple period. Are the ideas articulated in Mark's pericope designed for a Gentile audience, or were these ideas also espoused by Jews contemporary with or prior to Mark? If we

---

Borgen and Søren Giversen (Aarhus, Denmark: Aarhus University Press, 1995), 129. Reginald H. Fuller writes, "The word scribe is used in Hellenistic Greek for a lawyer in the wider sense (in Acts 13:35 it is used for a state official)" ("The Double Commandment of Love: A Test Case for the Criteria of Authenticity," in *Essays on the Love Commandment,* ed. Luise Schottroff et al. [Philadelphia: Fortress Press, 1978], 46).

[14] Furnish, *The Love Command in the New Testament,* 29. Johannes Nissen writes that "most scholars agree that the Gospel of Mark (12.28–34) has presented the love command as part of the early church's missionary preaching in Hellenistic society—in order to demonstrate the oneness of God against the many gods of Hellenism. The overall point is this: What is important for true religion is belief in and worship of the one God and obedience to the moral law, not religious ceremony of cultic performance" ("The Distinctive Character of the New Testament Love Command," 128–29).

can find evidence that Jews espoused these ideas, how might our conception of the intended audience for Mark's Gospel change?

Mark's *grammateus*: A wisdom figure or Jewish scribe?

Mark's overall portrayal of the scribes is negative. Most of them resist Jesus' teaching, test him with questions, and even plot his death. Just four verses after our pericope, Jesus bitterly denounces them: "Beware of the scribes.... They devour widows' houses and for the sake of appearance say long prayers. They will receive the greater condemnation" (Mark 12:38–40). Etienne Trocmé offers a plausible thesis for understanding this scribe in Mark 12:28–34 as exemplary among his contemporaries. He begins by noting the dominant role that the scribes play throughout Mark. They are mentioned more frequently in Mark than in the other Gospels, and they emerge as the primary opponents of Jesus and his teaching.[15] The scribes also oppose Jesus in both Matthew and Luke. But in Matthew they are generally associated with the Pharisees, who assume the dominant role among Jesus' enemies. In Luke, the scribes assume a less central role and are more associated with other religious groups opposing Jesus. In Mark, the scribes are among the instigators who attack Jesus, from his entrance into Jerusalem to the crucifixion (14:1, 43, 53; 15:1, 31). During that final week, the scribes are the main group that Jesus opposes in his counterattack (12:35; 12:38). The scribe in our pericope stands out among these: "One of them rallied in time to the winning side and thus escaped the judgment that fell on the group as a whole: he was the exception that proved the rule."[16]

The placement of the Mark 12:28–34 pericope is significant. The broader context from 11:27–12:40 consists of "controversy dialogues," which document Jesus' confrontation with various groups of Jewish leaders. Jesus emerges the victor in his disputes with the Sanhedrin group (11:27–33), the Pharisees and the Herodians (12:13–17), and the Sadducees (12:18–27). The scribe in 12:28–34 "converts" to Jesus' side and affirms Jesus' teaching on the Torah. Within this larger literary

---

[15] Etienne Trocmé, *The Formation of the Gospel according to Mark* (Philadelphia: Westminster Press, 1975), 94–95 (see p. 94, n. 2, for the statistics on scribes in Mark's Gospel as compared to Matthew, Luke, and John).

[16] Ibid., 96.

context, the placement of this section about a sympathetic scribe reflects the historical context of first-century Jewish-Christian polemic: "The meaning of the ordering of the text is clear: it is an appeal to the honest scribes to leave their authorities and organized parties in order to recognize the superiority of Jesus as an interpreter of Scripture and a representative of the best rabbinic tradition. It was a society for which Christianity represented a new party within Judaism which brought these four short passages together for the purposes of propaganda among the Jewish intellectual elite."[17]

Trocmé identifies the Jewish intellectual elite as the target audience of Mark's composition. Perhaps this readership could explain the "rationalistic" vocabulary that Mark uses in this pericope. In using this rational vocabulary, he may be seeking to appeal to a Hellenistic audience, but one that consists of Jews rather than Gentiles.

Hellenistic vocabulary in Mark?

Many terms in Mark's pericope are offered as evidence for the Gentile hypothesis. Terms such as "mind," "understanding," and "wisdom" would make the gospel appealing to rational Greeks. But in my opinion it is difficult to determine that these words would have been used solely to reach a Gentile audience. The language of the early Christian scriptures—both the Old Testament (LXX) and the emerging New Testament—was Greek. Thus, the early Christians' theology, ideas, and words were influenced by Hellenistic nomenclature.

Who determines what terms are distinctively Greek and what terms are distinctively Hebrew? Many Jews of the Diaspora, such as Philo, articulated the message of the Hebrew Bible using Greek language. Here, I think the identity of the scribe is relevant for assessing the weight we place on this "rationalistic" vocabulary. If Mark's scribe functions as a representative figure among his contemporaries, then perhaps his dialogue with Jesus is couched in terms that would present Jesus' teaching as a reasonable Jewish message, as Trocmé asserts in the above argument.

---

[17] Ibid., 97.

The law in Second Temple Judaism

Our story in Mark 12:28–34 begins with the scribe's question, "Which commandment is the first of all?" (12:28). Jesus answers with a first and a second. He declares that love of God and love of neighbor are the two greatest commandments in the Torah. The scribe enthusiastically endorses his summary and then adds that these two love commands are more important than "all whole burnt offerings and sacrifices" (v. 33).[18] In verse 34, Jesus commends the scribe for his insight.

Scholars who interpret this story as directed to a Gentile audience regard this summary as clearly emphasizing the moral law as opposed to the cultic or ritual law. But this summary of the law was not unprecedented in Judaism. Other rabbis and Jewish thinkers regarded the moral law (i.e., love for God and love for neighbor) as being of greater importance than the cultic law. Could Mark have been affirming a view of the law that some Jews who were not followers of Jesus would have affirmed?

The question of priority among the Torah commandments was not novel. Rabbis in antiquity were often asked to reduce the 613 commandments in the law (365 negative, 248 positive) into a single unifying principle or commandment. The best-known response came from Rabbi Hillel, who produced a negative form of the golden rule as a summarizing principle: "Do not do to your neighbor what is hateful to you; this is the whole Torah: the rest is commentary."[19] This statement corresponds to Jesus' second commandment about love for neighbor. Rabbi Akiba is even closer; he quotes Leviticus 19:18 verbatim: "But you shall love your neighbor as yourself. . . . This is the encompassing principle of the Law."[20] Neither of these two sources refers to the first commandment. A remark in Josephus, however, resembles the priority given to the love of God: "What, then, are the precepts and prohibitions of our Law? They are simple and familiar. The first (πρώτη) that leads (all commandments) concerns God."[21] These examples demonstrate

---

[18] The question is similar in Matthew: "Teacher, which commandment in the law is the greatest?" (Matt. 22:36). In Luke, however, a lawyer asks a different question: "Teacher, what must I do to inherit eternal life?" (Luke 10:25).

[19] b. Šabb. 31a.

[20] Sipra Lev. 200.

[21] Ag. Ap. 2.22 190.

that some Jewish leaders were giving similar summaries of the Torah. Furthermore, there are also antecedents to the juxtaposition of these two love commands.

The combination of love for God and love for neighbor is expressed in a few passages from the Old Testament Pseudepigrapha. In the book of *Jubilees* 36.3–7, the patriarch Isaac instructs his two sons to love each other ("your brothers") and to fear and worship God. These instructions mention brother rather than neighbor and command fear and worship rather than love for God; yet the text does bring together the two responsibilities: one toward brother and one toward God. A formulation much closer to that of Mark appears in the *Testaments of the Twelve Patriarchs*. In his instruction to his children, the patriarch Dan commands them: "Observe the Lord's commandments, then, my children, and keep his Law. Avoid wrath, and hate lying, in order that the Lord will dwell among you, and Beliar may flee from you. Each of you speak truth clearly to his neighbor, and do not fall into pleasure and troublemaking, and be at peace, holding to the God of peace. Thus no conflict will overwhelm you. Throughout all your life love the Lord, and one another with a true heart."[22]

This passage parallels Mark in combining love for God and one another. It commends loving one another "with a true heart," while in Mark loving with your heart is applied to God. Also, it serves as a summary of all the commandments and prohibitions that precede it in the list. But the formulation most similar to Mark's appears in Issachar's instructions to his children. In the following excerpt, love is commanded for both God and neighbor. The previous examples mentioned "brother" or "one another" but not neighbor: "Keep the Law of God, my children; achieve integrity; live without malice, not tinkering with God's commands or your neighbor's affairs. *Love the Lord and your neighbor*; be compassionate toward poverty and sickness."[23]

The works of Philo of Alexandria also include some notable examples. In *On the Life of Abraham*, while discussing the exemplary behavior of Abraham, Philo observes, "For the nature which is pious is also kindly, and the same person will exhibit both qualities, *holiness to God*

---

[22] T. Dan 5.1–3.

[23] T. Iss. 5:1–2 (my italics). Another excerpt from T. Iss. 7:6 is similar: "The Lord I loved with all my strength; likewise, I loved every human being as I love my children."

and justice to men."[24] He does not mention love, but he does classify human responsibilities using two categories: duties toward God and duties toward people. In another work, *The Special Laws,* Philo reduces the commandments in the law to two duties: "But among the vast number of particular truths and principles (in the Law) there studied, there stand out practically high above the others two main heads: *one of duty to God as shewn by piety and holiness, one of duty to men as shewn by humanity and justice,* each of them splitting up into multiform branches, all highly laudable."[25]

The foregoing examples from the Second Temple period indicate that the connection between love for God and love for brother or neighbor was in circulation before Jesus. Also, the recognition that these two duties summarized the law is attested by Philo. Thus, Jesus' formulation of the double love command was not novel, although it was unique in one respect; he alone *quoted* two particular commandments, while others only alluded to governing principles. There is no known Jewish precedent for this paired quotation of Deuteronomy 6:5 and Leviticus 19:18, but the idea that the Torah could be summarized with principles enjoining love of God and love of neighbor was articulated by several Jewish authors prior to Jesus.

I want to pursue a further line of comparison regarding the double love command. Dale C. Allison argues that the combination of these two commandments, love for God and love for neighbor, was recognized as a summary of the Ten Commandments among Christian and Jewish readers in the first century.[26] He traces this phenomenon to Philo, and specifically to *On the Decalogue.* First, Allison establishes that Philo regarded the Decalogue as a summary of the Torah.[27] Second, he argues that Philo believed the Decalogue itself could be summarized in two commandments.[28] These two command love for God and love for people; the former corresponds to the first five commands in the Deca-

---

[24] *Abraham* 208 (my italics).

[25] *Spec. Laws* 2.36 (my italics).

[26] Dale C. Allison Jr., "Mark 12.28-31 and the Decalogue," in *The Gospels and Scriptures of Israel,* ed. Craig A. Evans and William Richard Stegner (Sheffield, England: JSOT Press, 1994), 270-78.

[27] *Decalogue* 19-20; 154.

[28] *Decalogue* 50; 51; 106; 121.

logue and the latter corresponds to the second five commands in the Decalogue. Philo is encouraging his readers to love both God and people: "Now we have known some who associate themselves with one of the two sides (of the 10 commandments) and are seen to neglect the other.... These may be justly called lovers of men (who perform 2nd five), the former sort lovers of God (who perform 1st five). Both come but halfway in virtue; they only have it whole who win honour in both departments."[29]

Philo divides observers of the Decalogue into two types: φιλόθεοι (God lovers) and φιλάνθρωποι (people lovers). This division parallels Jesus' two commandments, to love God and to love neighbor, as expressed in Mark 12:28–34. Philo also recognizes a deficiency when only one of the two sides is performed, and not both. This recognition, too, is parallel to Jesus' understanding of the interdependence of the two love commands: "There is no other commandment (sing.) greater than these (pl.)" (Mark 12:31b). Furthermore, there is evidence that other Christians and Jews in the first century understood these two love commands similarly.

In his letter to the Romans (13:9), the Apostle Paul wrote, "The commandments, 'You shall not commit adultery; You shall not murder; You shall not steal; You shall not covet;' and any other commandment are summed up in this word, 'Love your neighbor as yourself.'" Paul lists here the commandments of the second half of the Decalogue and summarizes them with the quotation from Leviticus 19:18. In Matthew 19:16–19, Jesus lists the commandments from the second half of the Decalogue and then adds as a capstone, "You shall love your neighbor as yourself" (Matt. 19:19). This same summarizing idea is implicit in Mark.[30]

The first commandment to love God is inseparably linked with the Shema. Even in Deuteronomy, there is a connection between the Shema and the first five commands in the Decalogue, as Allison states: "Commentators often take the great imperative in the Shema (Deut. 6.4-5) to be a positive restatement of the Decalogue's first commandment."[31] This correlation is further attested by rabbinic sources dealing with the

---

[29] *Decalogue* 108–111.

[30] Allison, "Mark 12.28–31 and the Decalogue," 274.

[31] Ibid., 275.

recitation of the Shema with the Decalogue in the Jewish liturgy of the Second Temple period.[32] The Nash Papyrus (a Hebrew text dating from the first century BCE) juxtaposes the Shema and the Decalogue on a single sheet. At Qumran, the priest apparently recited the Decalogue and the Shema in conjunction, according to some tefillin fragments from 4QDeut^n.[33] Esther Eshel analyzes this text of 4QDeut^n and concludes that it is a collection of biblical passages used as a prayer book, containing among other things the Decalogue and Shema in juxtaposition.[34] In light of these Jewish sources, Allison concludes: "Thus the liturgical creed of the Jews in the New Testament period summarized the faith by quoting the ten commandments and the Shema. This is analogous to what I postulate for Mark 12:28–31: 'Hear, O Israel' and so on prefaces a summary of the Decalogue. In other words, *the profession in Mark is a restatement of the common Jewish profession, Jesus' creed was the Jewish creed.*"[35]

Thus, the double love command in Mark was not *necessarily* formulated for a Gentile audience, and it would certainly have fit well within the context of first-century Judaism. Mark's Jesus brought together the Shema and the Decalogue in a way that would have been familiar to orthodox Jews.

The idea that the moral law is more important than the cultic law was not novel either. The scribe in Mark 12:28–34 underscores the priority of the double love command over all "whole burnt offerings and sacrifices" (ὁλοκαυτωμάτων καὶ θυσιῶν). This phrase appears over one hundred times in the Septuagint.[36] The idea that the moral law is more important than the cultic law—that doing what is right is more important than doing a rite—was articulated consistently in the Old Testament. The prophets often emphasized this priority. The prophet/priest Samuel rebuked Saul: "Has the LORD as great delight in *burnt offer-*

---

[32] *m. Tam.* 5.1; *b. Ber.* 12a

[33] Esther Eshel, "4QDeut^n—A Text That Has Undergone Harmonistic Editing," *Hebrew Union College Annual* 62 (1991), ed. Herbert H. Paper (Cincinnati: Hebrew Union College, 1992), 122.

[34] Ibid., 123, 151–52.

[35] Dale C. Allison, "Mark 12.28–31 and the Decalogue," 276 (my italics).

[36] Craig A. Evans, *Mark 8:27–16:20*, Word Biblical Commentary, vol. 34B (Nashville: Thomas Nelson Publishers, 2001), 265.

ings and sacrifices (LXX: ὁλοκαυτώματα καὶ θυσίαι), as in obeying the voice of the LORD? Surely, to obey is better than sacrifice, and to heed than the fat of rams" (1 Sam. 15:22).

In another Old Testament text, the prophet Hosea declared, "For I desire steadfast love and not sacrifice (LXX: θυσίαν), the knowledge of God rather than burnt offerings (LXX: ὁλοκαυτώματα)." The resemblance to both Mark's idea and wording is striking (see also, for example, Isa. 1:11; Jer. 6:20; Amos 5:21–24).

A similar outlook was evident at Qumran. Joseph Baumgarten adduces two texts from the Qumran caves that articulate an analogous perspective on the cultic law. The first appears in 1QS 9:4, which predicts a time when the Qumran community will "atone for iniquitous guilt and for sinful unfaithfulness and as good will for the earth better than the flesh of burnt offerings and the fat of sacrifices." This passage looks forward to a time when the cultic law will be superseded, and like the Mark 12 text, it is phrased in a comparative way. Another text, 4Q266 10ⁱ, shows even greater similarity: "[The Messiah] will atone for their sin better than meal and sin offerings." This text is remarkable for its recognition that the Messiah, rather than cultic observance, is to be the source of atonement. Baumgarten remarks on these two texts: "Both envision a time when the perfection of priestly and lay institutions will become a source of atonement which will be available without the need for ritual sacrifice. In CD 14:19, it is the Messiah of Aaron and Israel, standing at the head of the total community, both priestly and lay, who will have the role of providing atonement."[37]

Mark may have expressed in Christian terms a similar attitude toward the temple and its sacrifices, in 12:33–34. As in the Qumran texts quoted above, he may have understood Jesus as the Messiah who would displace the temple as the source of atonement. After 70 CE, both Christians *and Jews* had to reevaluate their theology in light of the temple's destruction. Rabbi Yohanan ben Zakkai, who founded the academy at Yavneh, which became the basis for rabbinic Judaism, expressed an attitude similar to what we find in Mark. This excerpt, according to rabbinic tradition, is attributed to him: "Once as Rabban Johanan ben

---

[37] Joseph Baumgarten, "Messianic Forgiveness of Sin in CD 14:19 (4Q266 10 I 12–13)," in *Provo International Conference on the Dead Sea Scrolls*, ed. Donald W. Parry and Eugene Ulrich (Leiden: Brill, 1996), 541–42.

Zakkai was coming from Jerusalem, Rabbi Joshua followed after him and beheld the temple in ruins. 'Woe unto us!' Rabbi Joshua cried, 'that this, the place where the iniquities of Israel were atoned for, is laid waste!' 'My son,' Rabban Johanan said to him, 'be not grieved; we have another atonement as effective as this. And what is it? It is acts of loving-kindness, as it is said, "For I desire mercy and not sacrifice. """[38]

Thus, this priority given to the moral law in Mark does not *necessarily* reflect early Christian teaching to the Gentiles but was recognized among Jews in the period before and after the temple's ruin. The essence of the scribe's statement did not contradict the first-century Jewish perception of the demands of the Torah. All of this is to say that the double love command and the emphasis on the moral over the cultic law were not necessarily tailored to a Gentile audience.

Deuteronomy 6:4 in Second Temple Judaism

Mark's purpose in quoting the Shema was to stress God's oneness. The scribe's comment in verse 32, combining Deuteronomy 6:4b with Deuteronomy 4:35, affirms that "he is one, and besides him there is no other." In verse 34, Jesus commends this interpretation of the Shema. The meaning of the Shema in this pericope seems incontrovertible, but the question remains: was it quoted as a formula in the preaching to Gentiles, or did the author have a Jewish audience in mind?

What was the understanding of the Shema in ancient Judaism? E. P. Sanders recognizes a progression in Jewish thought concerning the worship of the God of Israel. Originally, the Shema, along with the first commandment of the Decalogue, was interpreted as a demand to worship the one true God, without a categorical denial of the existence of other gods.[39] However, as time passed, the interpretation of the Shema in Judaism narrowed its meaning to an assertion that the God of Israel is the only real god. Sanders concludes: "The Shema specifies that the Lord God is *one*, which in the first century implied strict monotheism: the one Lord is the only Lord."[40] Because this was the dominant

---

[38] 'Abot R. Nat. 4.5; 20a.

[39] E. P. Sanders, *Judaism: Practice and Belief 63 BCE– 66 CE* (Philadelphia: Trinity Press International, 1992), 242.

[40] Ibid., 242.

emphasis of the Shema in the Judaism contemporary with Mark, why would he quote it for a Jewish audience?

Joel Marcus offers a plausible explanation for Mark's use of the Shema as directed to a Jewish audience. He observes that the placement of this 12:28–34 pericope immediately before the one concerning David's son in 12:35–37 is significant. Mark quotes the Shema here, Marcus argues, to counterbalance the suggestion of 12:36–37 that as "David's Lord," Jesus will be enthroned beside God, a "two powers in heaven" (God and Christ) theology that could be seen as compromising God's unity. In early Christian-rabbinic debate, Jewish Christians defended both the unity of God and the quasi-divine status of Jesus against the charge of bi-theism. Marcus elaborates on Mark's intentions:

> The juxtaposition in 12.28–37 of the citation of the Shema with the allusion to a figure enthroned beside God is reminiscent of a series of rabbinic debates about the relation between God's oneness and heavenly intermediaries. In many of these debates Deut. 6:4, which A. Segal calls, 'the very center of the synagogue liturgy,' is marshaled against heretical notions of 'two powers in heaven.' It is probable that Deut. 6:4 performs a similar function in Mark 12:28–37, warding off any misunderstanding of Ps. 110:1 in the sense of bi-theism.[41]

Furthermore, Marcus recognizes an emphasis on a low Christology as a consistent theme throughout Mark's Gospel. In at least two other pericopes, 2:1–12 and 10:17–22, Mark upholds both the unity of God and the quasi-divine status of Jesus. In all three pericopes, 2:1–12, 10:17–22, and 12:28–34, the Greek adjective εἷς is used to modify God (2:7; 10:18; 12:29). The last reference is our quotation of the Shema, and in the other two, the Shema is probably implicit.[42] The context of the first passage involves Jesus' healing of a paralytic and then announcing that his sins are forgiven. Some of the scribes respond, "Why does this fel-

---

[41] Joel Marcus, *The Way of the Lord: Christological Exegesis of the Old Testament in the Gospel of Mark* (Louisville: John Knox Pess, 1992), 145. See also Alan F. Segal, *Two Powers in Heaven: Early Rabbinic Reports about Christianity and Gnosticism,* Studies in Judaism in Late Antiquity, vol. 25 (Leiden: Brill, 1977).

[42] Joel Marcus, "The Authority to Forgive Sins upon the Earth: The Shema in the Gospel of Mark," in *The Gospels and Scriptures of Israel,* ed. Evans and Stegner, 196.

low speak in this way? It is blasphemy! Who can forgive sins but *God alone* (εἷς)?" (Mark 2:7). Jesus responds by asserting that he has authority *on earth* to forgive sins (2:10), thus implying that his authority is derived from the one God *in heaven*.

The context of the second passage involves an exchange between the rich man and Jesus.[43] The rich man addresses him with the title "Good Teacher," which provokes Jesus' retort, "Why do you call me good? No one is good but *God alone* (εἷς)" (Mark 10:18). Jesus' response implies a distance between himself and God. Marcus elaborates on this threefold repetition of εἷς and its significance for Mark: "If an adjective were felt to be necessary to underline God's unique goodness and power to forgive sins, then the natural candidate would be μονος (alone), as in Luke 5.21, rather than εἷς. Why then does Mark have εἷς in these two places (2.7 & 10.18)? The most logical response would seem to run: it is the key-word of the Shema."[44]

This view is reinforced by the linguistic resemblance of Mark's usage to that of Paul in 1 Corinthians 8:6 (εἷς θεός), which also appears to be an allusion to the Shema.[45] Thus, Marcus provides a credible interpretation of Mark's use of the Shema. It is a theory that considers the broader context of the entire Gospel of Mark and fits well within the context of first-century Jewish-Christian debate. This concern for affirming both God's oneness and Jesus' exalted status is a consistent theme in Mark's Gospel, as evidenced by these three stories.

Conclusions

Why, then, did Mark quote Deuteronomy 6:4 as a preface to the double love command? The first section of this essay laid out the dominant hypothesis among scholars regarding this question: it was quoted for a Gentile audience. Several unique features in Mark's pericope are interpreted in defense of this theory. The second part scrutinized this hypothesis by examining each of these features from a Jewish perspective. I determined that each of these features in Mark could as plausibly be directed toward a Jewish audience.

---

[43] Bultmann also labels this exchange a scholastic dialogue (*The History of the Synoptic Tradition*, 54).

[44] Marcus, "The Authority to Forgive Sins upon the Earth," 198.

[45] Ibid., 198.

What shall we conclude? I do not intend to displace the previous hypothesis with an entirely different one; instead, I propose a synthesis of the two perspectives. However, I regard the overall framework of Mark 12:28–34 as directed toward a Jewish audience, contending (along the lines argued by Marcus and Trocmé) that Mark quoted the Shema for the benefit of Jewish readers.

Joel Marcus posits that Mark quoted the Shema to counter the Jewish charge of bi-theism. Mark needed to maintain a delicate balance between Jesus' exalted status and God's oneness. This theme permeates the Gospel of Mark. Mark is generally recognized as having the lowest Christology of the four Gospels. In addition to the three passages cited above (2:1–12; 10:17–22; 12:28–34), several other Markan texts indicate this concern (see 10:40; 14:36; 15:34). The clearest statement in Mark countering any charge of bi-theism appears in 13:32: "But about that day or hour no one knows, neither the angels in heaven, *nor the Son*, but only the Father." Mark is careful to maintain a distance between God and Jesus. Thus, Marcus's notion that Mark quotes the Shema in its larger context as defense against Jewish charges is most plausible, because it is most comprehensive. I affirm that Mark's pericope was designed for apologetic purposes, but his apology was directed to a Jewish milieu, as opposed to a Gentile one.

Etienne Trocmé's interpretation of the scribe in 12:28–34 offers a different slant. He also views the scribe as a representative figure, but one within the *Jewish* wisdom tradition. This sympathetic scribe appeals to his Jewish colleagues to recognize Jesus as a great rabbi. Again, the apologetic purpose is maintained. But the rationalistic vocabulary is understood to be addressed to a Jewish intellectual elite.

Thus, Mark quoted Deuteronomy 6:4 for apologetic reasons. He intended to affirm God's oneness, but he did so to present Jesus' teaching as in continuity with orthodox Judaism. This premise is further supported by Jesus' affirming dialogue with the scribe, a Jew who presents Jesus' teaching as being in continuity with orthodox Judaism.

Certain features in Mark's account do seem to be tailored to a Hellenistic audience. One such feature is the presence of distinctively rationalistic vocabulary, such as διάνοια (mind) and νουνεχῶς (wisely). However, such terminology would have appealed not only to Gentiles but also to Hellenists (Greek-speaking Jews) and other Diaspora Jews who had undergone some assimilation to Greco-Roman culture. The recognition that Mark's scribe is a seeker of wisdom does not imply that he is Greek; the Jews also had a wisdom tradition. These two insights into Mark's pericope (rationalistic vocabulary and the scribe as a wisdom figure) are valid. But my contention is that these elements were formulated not for a Gentile audience but for a Hellenistic Jewish one.

CHAPTER THREE

The significance of love of God and neighbor in Luke's Gospel

Jeff T. Williams

Throughout Christian history, the ethical requirements for followers of Jesus have been summarized as love of God and love of neighbor. The tradition of pairing these two love commandments is attributable to the fact that all three synoptic Gospels record Jesus as combining them. Both commands are drawn from the Old Testament (OT), and scholars have long studied the question of whether Jews of Jesus' time used these two commandments to summarize the Torah. What scholars have often overlooked, however, is that Luke has gone a step further than even the other Synoptics. Instead of merely juxtaposing the two OT commandments, the Gospel of Luke collapses them into one command. This paper seeks to examine the significance of including love of God and love of neighbor in a single command.

The questions scholars commonly ask regarding the double commandment of the Synoptics are by no means irrelevant to the present discussion. It matters what sources Luke used in framing his narrative. The extent to which love of God and love of neighbor were commonly connected in Second Temple Judaism directly affects the significance of Luke's one command. Moreover, what love of neighbor meant during this time is also important if we are to ascertain the significance of the one command in Luke 10:25–37.

Our analysis begins with a brief study of the sources behind Luke 10:25–27, to understand the nature of the pericope in general and the one command in particular. Second, we will explore the extent to which love of God and love of neighbor were connected in Second Temple Judaism. This demonstration of the uniqueness of the one-command formulation in its historical context will enable us to approach Luke 10 anew. Returning to an examination of Luke 10:25–37, we will investigate the purpose to which Luke has used the one-command formulation. We will then be in a position to determine the significance of the one command in Luke 10:25–37.

LUKE 10:25–28 AND ITS SOURCES

The synoptic Gospels

Opinions abound concerning the use of the sources Mark and Q in Luke 10:25–28. Some scholars argue that Luke has reworked the Mark account, probably to give an appropriate introduction to the parable of the good Samaritan which follows.[1] Others argue that Luke is not using Mark but Q.[2] Still others contend that Luke uses both sources,[3] and others that Luke uses neither.[4] This latter position is perhaps the most widely held, but it would be an overstatement to say that a scholarly consensus exists on the matter.

A close comparison of Luke and the other Synoptics reveals why the matter of Luke's sources is such a difficult issue. While the account in Luke displays some large-scale similarities with that in Matthew and Mark, the context of Luke's account and Luke's vocabulary and grammar diverge so much from that of Matthew and Mark that the relationship between them is complex, to say the least.

---

[1] For example, Filip Noël, "The Double Commandment of Love in Lk 10,27: A Deuteronomistic Pillar or Lukan Redaction of Mk 12, 29–33?" in *The Scriptures in the Gospels,* ed. C. M. Tuckett (Louvain, Belgium: Leuven University Press, 1997), 559–70.

[2] Arland J. Hultgren appeals to a consensus that Luke 10:25–28 does not use Mark at all, but rather Q and L. See Hultgren, "The Double Commandment of Love in Mt 22:34–40: Its Sources and Composition," *Catholic Biblical Quarterly* 36 (1974): 373. A quick perusal of the research on this matter reveals that no such consensus exists.

[3] For example, see Reginald H. Fuller, "The Double Commandment of Love: A Test Case for the Criteria of Authenticity," in *Essays on the Love Commandment,* ed. Luise Schottroff, trans. Reginald H. Fuller and Ilse Fuller (Philadelphia: Fortress Press, 1978), 41–56.

[4] Among those who argue that Luke was following an independent version of the story are I. Howard Marshall, *The Gospel of Luke: A Commentary on the Greek Text,* The New International Greek Testament Commentary (Grand Rapids: Eerdmans, 1978), 440–41; Joseph A. Fitzmyer, *The Gospel according to Luke (X–XXIV),* The Anchor Bible, vol. 28A (Garden City, NY: Doubleday, 1985), 877–78; and Charles A. Kimball, *Jesus' Exposition of the Old Testament in Luke's Gospel* (Sheffield, England: Sheffield Academic Press, 1994), 120–21.

I. Howard Marshall describes the relationship between Luke 10:25–27 and Mark 12:28–34 as a "crucial problem."[5] Luke's text displays enough similarity with Mark's account to show that he is familiar with Mark, yet there are enough differences to raise questions about whether Luke is following Mark at this point. On the larger scale, both narratives rely on Deuteronomy 6:5 and Leviticus 19:18 as a way to encapsulate the law.[6] It is harder, however, to find specific similarities in vocabulary and grammar. Both Mark and Luke include four faculties with which people are to love God. And they include the same four: καρδία (heart), ψυχή, (soul), ἰσχύς (strength—which Matthew does not use), and διανοία (mind). However, Luke and Mark differ in the order of these four faculties. Luke agrees with Mark in the use of the preposition ἐξ (from, with) before the first faculty, although only here (of the four prepositions used to refer to the four faculties) does Luke use the preposition Mark uses. Like Mark, Luke puts the double command in the mouth of the scribe, although in Mark it first comes from the mouth of Jesus. I will argue that this element is an example of Luke's use of Mark, despite the fact that the later interchange between the scribe and Jesus in Mark is completely different from the interchange related in Luke.

These similarities are difficult to analyze, because each seems to be qualified by the differences surrounding it. Compared with the differences, there are few similarities in Mark and Luke. A major difference between Luke, on one hand, and Mark and Matthew, on the other, is that Luke places the narrative in an entirely different period of Jesus' ministry. For Mark and Matthew, it occurs while Jesus is in Jerusalem. Luke, on the other hand, places this narrative on the way to Jerusalem, a major literary section in his Gospel. Luke does include the narratives that occur immediately before and after this one in Matthew and Mark. Had he retained the order of Matthew and Mark, Luke would have placed this narrative after Luke 20:40. Instead, it appears ten chapters earlier.

---

[5] Marshall, *The Gospel of Luke*, 440.

[6] Although the first question is very different in Luke than in Mark or Matthew, we are clearly still dealing with the matter of one's reading of the law. Marshall explains that the phrase πῶς ἀναγινώσκεις "reflects Jewish methods of argumentation" (ibid., 443). It clearly refers to the law and may be rendered, "How do you read it?"

We observe a number of other significant differences between Luke and Mark. The chief instigator in the story is described as a νομικός (lawyer) in Luke and as a γραμματεύς (scribe) in Mark. The lawyer in Luke is described in hostile terms, as one testing Jesus, while in Mark the scribe is depicted as sincere. The instigating question itself is different. In fact, except for the similarities mentioned above, everything about the interchange between Jesus and the lawyer is different in Luke. Finally, Mark separates the two love commands in the double commandment, while Luke combines them. For purposes of this paper, this difference is important.

Luke and Matthew, on the other hand, have in common more aspects of the story. Both Matthew and Luke describe the instigator as a lawyer attempting to test Jesus.[7] In both accounts, the lawyer addresses Jesus in the same way: διδάσκαλε (teacher). Both deal with what is ἐν τῷ νόμῳ (in the law), although the questions posed to Jesus in the two accounts are quite different. Matthew and Luke omit Mark's inclusion of the beginning of the Shema. Concerning the command to love God, Matthew has only three descriptors. All three are similar to Luke's, although the order more closely resembles Mark's. Matthew and Luke agree on the preposition used, ἐν (in), on two occasions (as opposed to Mark's use of ἐξ).

While Luke and Matthew display more explicit connections than do Luke and Mark, they also exhibit puzzling differences. These differences give us pause in asserting Matthew, or Q, to be Luke's primary source for this narrative. We have already mentioned that Luke differs from Matthew in using ἐξ instead of ἐν before one of the faculties, and in including a fourth faculty, ἰσχύς Most of the other differences have been mentioned in regard to Luke's differences with Mark. Included among these is the fact that Luke differs from Matthew in the formulation of the double love command. Both Matthew and Mark order the two commands in some way, as first and second or as greatest and second. In Luke, they are fused into one command.

We are left with a puzzle. At points, Luke agrees with Matthew over against Mark. At other points, Luke sides with Mark over against Matthew. Even if one argues that Luke has used both Mark and Mat-

---

[7] The words used here are slightly different. Matthew uses πειράζων αὐτόν (testing him) while Luke uses ἐκπειράζων αὐτὸν (testing him).

thew, one must postulate another extensive source that might account for the shape of Luke's narrative, or one may simply conclude that Luke is narrating a different story altogether. I find this last step unsatisfactory, because the common elements in the stories suggest that Luke is reworking the narrative that we find in both Mark and Matthew. There are just enough similarities to support the argument that Luke is using both Mark and Q.[8] Therefore, it seems more likely that Luke has taken the Mark and Q accounts of this narrative and reworked them around a particular narrative structure, one that is also found in Luke 18:18–25.

Luke 18:18–25: A parallel narrative

A number of scholars see Luke drawing on the narrative structure of Luke 18 in shaping the narrative on the double command. Both narratives are framed by the initial question: τί ποιήσας ζωὴν αἰώνιον κληρονομήσω; ("What must I do to inherit eternal life?"). In light of the drastic difference between this question and the instigating questions found in Mark (and presumably in Q), it seems reasonable to suppose that Luke has drawn the question from the narrative in Luke 18, itself from the Markan tradition, in order to place the two narratives on parallel planes.[9]

---

[8] It is traditional to name as Q those similarities between Matthew and Luke that are not in Mark. There is much debate about whether this passage is in Q. *The Critical Edition of Q* in the Hermeneia series argues that it is not—although it does not rank its decision very highly (see *The Critical Edition of Q: Synopsis Including the Gospels of Matthew and Luke, Mark and Thomas with English, German, and French Translations of Q and Thomas*, ed. James M. Robinson, Paul Hoffmann, and John S. Kloppenborg [Minneapolis: Fortress Press, 2000], 200–203). That discussion is just a way of talking about whether Luke and Matthew have enough similarities to hypothesize a common source (as opposed to Mark). It seems to me that there enough such similarities, and thus we can conclude that this account was in Q—whatever form Q might have had.

[9] Thomas E. Phillips also argues that the narratives in Luke 10 and Luke 18 are made parallel so each informs the other's content. See Phillips, "Subtlety as a Literary Technique in Luke's Characterization of Jews and Judaism," in *Literary Studies in Luke-Acts: Essays in Honor of Joseph B. Tyson,* ed. Richard P. Thompson and Thomas E. Phillips (Macon, GA: Mercer University Press, 1998), 313–26. But his conclusion—that Jesus is engaging in a critique of the notion that one must "do" something in order to "inherit" eternal life—seems improbable to me. In the larger scope of Luke, Jesus expects his followers to adhere to the commands set out in these two sections.

One observes other significant similarities in the two narratives. In both, Jesus is addressed as διδάσκαλε, although the Luke 18 narrative adds the adjective ἀγαθέ (good). Both narratives supply an answer about the law. That is, both offer a law summary as the way to eternal life.[10] In both narratives, that summary is questioned.[11] In both narratives, Jesus proceeds to expound on the law summary, defining its meaning in an offensive or challenging way.[12]

Because Luke borrowed the introductory question from the story of the rich ruler to preface his account of the double commandment, we should expect that the content of these two narratives in Luke will also be parallel to some degree. That parallelism will be fleshed out later in this essay. For now, we note that the influence of Luke 18:18–25 accounts for the major differences between Luke 10:25–27 and its parallels in Mark and Q.[13] We conclude, then, that Luke has taken material from Mark and Q and reworked it to parallel the story in Luke 18:18–25.

The nature of Luke's one command

It is worth taking a moment to consider Luke's source for the one command. Clearly, Luke's source for the content of the two commands,

---

[10] In Luke 10, the law is summarized by the one command: love God and neighbor. In Luke 18, the law is summarized using various commandments from the Decalogue, with the probable intent to refer to all of the Decalogue or at least to the last six, the ones dealing with the ethical treatment of other human beings.

[11] In Luke 10, the summary is challenged by the question, "Who is my neighbor?" In Luke 18, the challenge is implied. There, the ruler insists that he is already obeying (his sense of) the commandments of the Decalogue. His challenge is an implied form of the question "What else?" or "Is there more to these commands than I think?"

[12] In Luke 10, this challenge occurs in the parable of the good Samaritan. In Luke 18, the offense comes in the command of Jesus to sell all, give to the poor, and follow.

[13] Neither Luke 18 nor Mark/Q seems to be the source of Jesus' response in verse 28. Some suggest that Luke here draws from Leviticus 18:5, which also makes use of some of the key terms. That theory fits with the lawyer's opening question about eternal life. See Eduard Verhoef, "(Eternal) Life and Following the Commandments: Lev 18,5 and Luke 10,28," in *The Scriptures in the Gospels,* ed. Tuckett, 571–77; and William Richard Stegner, "The Parable of the Good Samaritan and Leviticus 18:5," in *The Living Text: Essays in Honor of Ernest W. Saunders,* ed. Dennis E. Groh and Robert Jewett (Lanham, MD: University Press of America, 1985), 27–38. Stegner argues that Lev. 18:5 allows for the parable to be considered an original part of the larger unity, not as a secondary addition. No connection will be made to this possible source of Luke in this essay.

love of God and love of neighbor, is the material from Mark (and the Septuagint [LXX], which Mark draws on) and Q. Luke, however, has collapsed both parts of the command into one, so that love of God and love of neighbor appears to be one action—one specific loving act. But neither Mark, nor Q, nor Luke 18 can account for the curious form of the command found in Luke 10:27. This unique formulation, then, must be attributed to Luke's own hand.

One might challenge this assumption by asking whether this formulation was already present in Q, a source we have already concluded Luke drew from in constructing this narrative. This is a question of whether Luke or Matthew more faithfully represents Q at this point. I agree with Jan Lambrecht that the fact that Luke has fused two OT quotations and put them in the mouth of the lawyer (instead of Jesus) suggests that the Lukan text is less original than that of either Mark or Matthew.[14] This argument is strengthened by the fact that the Lukan narrative has been shaped by material that is widely held to be specifically Lukan, the parable of the good Samaritan. Therefore, it seems most probable that the formulation of the one command in Luke 10:27 is a specific Lukan redaction of an inherited tradition. That conclusion leads one to ask: Why has Luke formed the double love command tradition in this way? What purpose does it serve in the larger narrative of Luke 10:25–37? To address these questions, we need to know whether this formulation was unique to Jesus.

IS LUKE'S ONE-COMMAND FORMULATION UNIQUE?

In attempting to ascertain the significance of Luke's formulation of the double love command as one command, one must do more than determine that it came from Luke's own hand rather than from the inherited tradition. That conclusion demonstrates some form of intentionality, but it leaves the door open to the possibility that such an assertion was commonplace in Luke's day. That such a formulation or connection was commonplace does not of course preclude the possibility that Luke intentionally redacted the tradition for a particular purpose. But if Luke's formulation and connection were commonplace, the impact on

---

[14] Jan Lambrecht, *Once More Astonished: The Parables of Jesus* (New York: Crossroad, 1981), 64. Lambrecht uses this reasoning specifically to distinguish the Lukan text from the Markan one. I have simply transferred his reasoning to argue that at this point Matthew is likely more true to Q than is Luke.

readers is substantially altered, as is the effect on the narrative of Luke 10:25–37. Therefore, we look now at whether Luke's formulation of one command was unique to him.

Connecting love of God and love of neighbor in Second Temple Judaism

The period of Second Temple Judaism forms the basic historical context of Luke's Gospel, although it was written soon after the destruction of the temple (70 CE). The purpose of this section is to explore the extent to which love of God and love of neighbor were connected during that period. Closely linked to this exploration is the question whether love of God and love of neighbor were understood together to be an adequate summation of the law.

Scholars disagree about these issues. Some regard the Synoptics as advocating nothing out of the ordinary in their summary of the law as love of God and neighbor. But the evidence does not support their conclusion. Furthermore, the evidence indicates that Luke's formulation of one command is nothing short of groundbreaking and unique.

E. P. Sanders argues that it was quite common in Second Temple Judaism to understand love of God and love of neighbor together as encompassing the law. His case rests on two central sources, the writings of Philo and the so-called *Letter of Aristeas*.[15] John Nolland similarly concludes that "the Gospel identification of the first and second commandments is thoroughly at home in a first-century Palestinian Jewish setting."[16] His central sources are the *Testaments of the Twelve Patriarchs*, part of the Old Testament Pseudepigrapha. Do these sources justify the claims that Sanders, Nolland, and others make?

Philo, a Jewish apologist and philosopher, was a Diaspora Jew who lived in Alexandria. He was a contemporary of Jesus and Paul, and his writings remain important sources for understanding Hellenistic Judaism in the first century. As David M. Scholer observes, Philo's writings demonstrate the "multifaceted character of Second Temple Judaism."[17]

---

[15] For Sanders's argument on this point, see *Judaism: Practice and Belief, 63 BCE–66 CE* (London: SCM Press, 1992), 230–35, 257–60.

[16] John Nolland, *Luke 9:21–18:34*, Word Biblical Commentary, vol. 35B, ed. David A. Hubbard and Glenn W. Barker (Dallas: Word Books, 1993), 582.

[17] David M. Scholer, foreword to *The Works of Philo: Complete and Unabridged*, trans. C. D. Yonge (Peabody, MA: Hendrickson Publishers, 1993), xiii.

Certainly, his work betrays a strong Hellenistic influence and therefore displays a way of thinking quite foreign to some Jewish writings of this period.

In *On the Virtues*, Philo observes the close connection between two virtues, piety and humanity: "We must now proceed in due order to consider that virtue which is more nearly related to piety, being as it were a sister, a twin sister, namely, humanity, which the father of our laws loved so much that I know not if any human being was ever more attached to it."[18] That sentiment is echoed and expounded in Philo's *On the Life of Abraham*: "That is enough to say about the piety of a man, though there is a vast abundance of other things which might be brought forward in praise of it. We might also investigate his skill and wisdom as displayed towards his fellow men; for it belongs to the same character to be pious towards God and affectionate towards man; and both these qualities, of holiness towards God and justice towards man, are commonly seen in the same individual."[19]

In this writing, "justice" is used to summarize one's ethical obligations to other people. As in the above quotations, Philo closely connects it to piety. In *On the Special Laws*, Philo both connects these two kinds of ethical obligations and refers to them as the most important of our obligations: "And there are, as we may say, two most especially important heads of all the innumerable particular lessons and doctrines; the regulating of one's conduct towards God by the rules of piety and holiness, and of one's conduct towards men by the rules of humanity and justice; each of which is subdivided into a great number of subordinate ideas, all praiseworthy."[20] Still, none of the above passages actually deals with the law; they do not summarize or encapsulate the Torah.

Philo does address the written law in *On the Decalogue*. He observed, as have many others, that the Ten Commandments may be divided into two sections: those that deal with duty to God and those that deal with duty to other humans. In this context, Philo again connects the two chief duties of people:

---

[18] *Virtues* 51 (ibid., 644).

[19] *Abraham* 208 (ibid., 428).

[20] *Spec. Laws* 2.63 (ibid., 574).

Now, one may properly call both these latter, these philan-
thropic men, and also the former class, the lovers of God, but
half perfect in virtue; for those only are perfect who have a good
reputation in both points: but those who do not attend to their
duties towards men so as to rejoice with them at their common
blessings, or to grieve with them at events of a contrary character, and who yet do not devote themselves to piety and holiness
towards God, may be thought to have changed into the nature of
wild beasts, the very preeminence among whom, in point of fe-
rocity, those are entitled to who neglect their parents, being hostile to both the divisions of virtue above mentioned, namely,
piety towards God, and their duty towards men.[21]

From these passages in Philo's writings, what can we conclude
about the connection of love of God and neighbor in the Synoptics? We
can conclude that understanding one's ethical obligations in terms of
two main duties—piety and justice—was not uncommon. Still, Philo's
observations are couched in terms of Greek virtues and are hardly to be
understood as summaries of the Torah. The last quotation from *On the
Decalogue* comes closest, but its language is far from that of the Synoptics and the Septuagint. Philo's language is that of piety and justice;[22]
the Synoptics speak of love of God and love of neighbor.[23] They are
worlds apart. Philo does not appeal to Deuteronomy 6:5 or Leviticus
19:18, nor does he suggest any reading of the law. Finally, he clearly
separates the duties of piety and justice. Although he maintains that we
must do both (a point that will later be significant for the present argument), he understands them as distinct duties. He nowhere comes
close to the one-command formulation found in Luke 10.

The *Letter of Aristeas* is an ancient document primarily about the
translation of the Hebrew Bible into Greek. The dating of the document
is difficult, although it almost certainly is earlier than the synoptic
Gospels. It is no earlier than 270 BCE and no later than the writing of
Josephus' *Antiquities*. Moses Hadas cautiously dates the letter around

---

[21] *Decalogue* 110 (ibid., 528).

[22] For "love," Philo uses φιλανθρώους and φιλοθέους, both thoroughly Hellenistic terms.

[23] The Synoptics follow the LXX in using a form of ἀγαπάω to express their notion of love.

130 BCE.[24] The document makes no explicit reference to the Decalogue, but it asserts that Moses "in the first place laid down the principles of piety and justice and expounded them point by point."[25] The language is Hellenistic, using words such as "piety" and "justice," as in Philo.

Two other sections are important to Sanders's argument. The first is a Jewish sage's response to King Ptolemy, who had asked for advice on maintaining his kingdom "unimpaired to the end." The sage counsels the king: "You would maintain it best by imitating the constant gentleness of God. For by exercising long-suffering patience and dealing with those who merit punishment more gently than they deserve, you will turn them from wickedness and bring them to repentance."[26] The second section reads thus: "In every way, Your Majesty, you must make piety the objective of whatever you say and do, so that you may be certain in your own mind that, adhering to virtue, you do not choose to grant favors contrary to reason nor, abusing your power, set justice aside."[27] From these texts Sanders concludes, "The person who governs his actions by 'piety' will uphold 'virtue' and will never transgress 'justice.' Love of God and of neighbor were seen as inseparable; so Jews taught one another and, when they had the chance, others who would listen."[28]

Sanders overstates his case. Like Philo's writings, the *Letter of Aristeas* offers little to the discussion at hand other than demonstrating that the Greek virtues of piety and justice were seen as encompassing the whole duty of humanity. It is a far cry from such an assertion to arguing that Deuteronomy 6:5 and Leviticus 19:18 summarize the entire law, and that they can be understood as a single command.

The *Testaments of the Twelve Patriarchs* offers language that is much more similar to that of the Synoptics. At first glance, this source seems to support Sanders's and Nolland's conclusion that the double love commands in the Synoptics were common in their historical context.

---

[24] For an extensive discussion on the dating of the *Letter of Aristeas*, see Moses Hadas, ed. and trans., *Aristeas to Philocrates (Letter of Aristeas)* (New York: KTAV Publishing House, 1973), 3–54.

[25] *Let. Aris.* 130 (ibid., 153).

[26] *Let. Aris.* 188 (ibid., 175).

[27] *Let. Aris.* 215 (ibid., 184).

[28] Sanders, *Judaism*, 185.

But a close examination reveals a need for caution. Moreover, the questions of dating and Christian interpolations cast doubts about whether these texts qualify as evidence in the present discussion.

The most startling similarities to the Synoptics are found in two testaments, *Issachar* and *Dan*. The *Testament of Issachar* 5:1–3 reads thus:

> Keep the Law of God, my children;
> achieve integrity; live without malice,
> not tinkering with God's commands or your neighbor's affairs.
> Love the Lord and your neighbor;[29]
> be compassionate toward poverty and sickness.
> Bend your back in farming,
> perform the tasks of the soil in every kind of agriculture,
> offering gifts gratefully to the Lord.[30]

Here love of the Lord and love of neighbor are combined in a single sentence, in a way similar to what we find in Luke 10. A connection between loving God and loving human beings is also made in *Issachar* 7:2–7:

> I have not had intercourse with any woman other than my wife,
> nor was I promiscuous by lustful look.
> I did not drink wine to the point of losing self-control.
> I was not passionately eager for any desirable possession
>   of my neighbor.
> There was no deceit in my heart;
> no lie passed through my lips.
> I joined in lamentation with every oppressed human being,
> and shared my bread with the poor.
> I did not eat alone; I did not transgress boundaries;
> I acted in piety and truth all my days.
> The Lord I loved with all my strength;
> likewise, I loved every human being as I love my children.[31]

---

[29] The Greek reads: ἀγαπήσατε τὸν Κύριον καὶ τὸν πλησίον. Taken from R. H. Charles, ed., *The Greek Versions of the Testaments of the Twelve Patriarchs* (Oxford: Clarendon, 1908), 112.

[30] H. C. Kee, trans., *Testaments of the Twelve Patriarchs*, in *The Old Testament Pseudepigrapha*, vol. 1, ed. James H. Charlesworth (Garden City, NY: Doubleday, 1983), 803.

[31] This translation follows one of two possible readings in the Greek: τὸν Κύριον

You do these as well, my children,
and every spirit of Beliar will flee from you,
and no act of human evil will have power over you.
Every wild creature you shall subdue,
so long as you have the God of heaven with you,
and walk with all mankind in sincerity of heart.[32]

A final applicable text is found in the *Testament of Dan* 5:1–4. Here again, love of God and love of one another are combined in one command:

Observe the Lord's commandments, then, my children,
and keep his Law.
Avoid wrath,
and hate lying,
in order that the Lord may dwell among you,
and Beliar may flee from you.
Each of you should speak truth clearly to his neighbor,
and do not fall into pleasure and troublemaking,
but be at peace, holding to the God of peace.
Thus no conflict will overwhelm you.
Throughout all your life love the Lord,
and one another with a true heart.[33]

For I know that in the last days you will defect from the Lord,
you will be offended at Levi,
and revolt against Judah;
but you will not prevail over them.

ἠγάπησα ἐν πάσῃ ἰσχύι μου ὁμοίως καὶ πάντα ἄνθρωπον ἠγάπησα ὑπὲρ τὰ τέκνα μου (Charles, *Greek Versions of the Testaments of the Twelve Patriarchs*, 115). The other possible reading is quite different: τὸν Κύριον ἠγάπησα καὶ πάντα ἄνθρωπον ἐξ ὅλης τῆς καρδίας (ibid., 115). Both readings have some similarities to Luke 10 that the other does not. Note that this second reading again combines love of the Lord and of humans into a single clause.

[32] Kee, *Testaments of the Twelve Patriarchs*, 804.

[33] The Greek reads: ἀγαπήσατε τὸν Κύριον ἐν πάσῃ τῇ ζωῇ ὑμῶν καὶ ἀλλήλους ἐν ἀληθινῇ καρδίᾳ (Charles, *Greek Versions of the Testaments of the Twelve Patriarchs*, 137).

An angel of the Lord guides them both,
because by them Israel shall stand.[34]

What conclusions can be drawn from these excerpts? First, the language of these texts clearly differs from the language of Philo and the *Letter of Aristeas*. It is much more similar to the language of the Synoptics. Moreover, we see that in these texts the love of God is paired frequently with the love of other humans. We even have them combined into one command. We might be inclined to conclude, as Nolland does, that what we have in the Synoptics and even Luke 10 is not unique in its historical context.

There are many reasons, however, to be cautious about such a conclusion. First, there are many differences between the Synoptics' double love command and what appears in the testaments. While love of God and love of other humans are connected in the testaments, they always appear in the context of a larger list of exhortations. That is, they do not stand alone, and by no means are they understood by themselves to summarize the law. Also, it is clear that we do not have the combination of two particular OT texts, Deuteronomy 6:5 and Leviticus 19:18, because a different form of the verb ἀγαπάω (to love) is used in them. The testaments use the aorist imperative, while the Synoptics follow the LXX in using the future indicative. Of the three quotations cited above, only once was the reference to love of neighbor (πλησίον). Moreover, the way these two kinds of love are combined into a single clause in these texts differs from how they are combined in Luke 10. The formulations here are not meant to be read as one command. Rather, an ellipsis is employed, with the verb being implied in the second part of the phrase.[35] Thus, love of God and neighbor are not really combined into one command in these texts. Rather, the author has chosen not to repeat the verb a second time.

In using the *Testaments of the Twelve Patriarchs* as a source for Second Temple Judaism, however, an even greater dilemma blocks our way. How reliable is a pre–70 CE dating for the texts that we have today? It is common knowledge that the texts as we have them contain Christian interpolations. Is this fact devastating to their credibility?

---

[34] Kee, *Testaments of the Twelve Patriarchs*, 809.

[35] On criteria for establishing the presence of an ellipsis, see the discussion below on whether what we have in Luke 10 is an ellipsis (pages 90–91).

Nolland briefly suggests that we have no reason to doubt the pre-Christian origin of these texts, and he does little to argue his case.[36] He assumes that the testaments are essentially Jewish documents, and that the Christian interpolations can be readily identified and distinguished from the rest. This is also the position of H. C. Kee, who dates the testaments to around 150 BCE.[37]

Marinus de Jonge, on the other hand, has argued persuasively that these texts cannot be considered Jewish at all. He contends that they are Christian texts dating from around 200 CE. He acknowledges that the testaments are based on Jewish documents, but he argues that the material in its present form has been so thoroughly reworked that it should be considered Christian, not Jewish.[38] That is, we have no way to extract the Christian interpolations from the text, leaving behind a Second Temple Jewish source.

A challenge to this thesis comes from Qumran. While there had been several other Semitic fragments of material similar to the testaments, Qumran has yielded many more. In 1996, Greenfield and Stone published the Aramaic Levi Document (ALD), a collection of fragments from cave 4 that bore similarities to material in the *Testament of Levi*. Could this document constitute evidence demonstrating the pre-Christian existence of the testaments? De Jonge notes that there is without doubt some connection between the ALD and the *Testament of Levi*. He further observes, "At the same time, comparing *T. Levi* with ALD brings out interesting Christian elements in the testament, which are structural rather than incidental and can, therefore, not be eliminated as later interpolations."[39] De Jonge concludes that there are no *Testaments of the Twelve Patriarchs* at Qumran. All that we have from Levi and

---

[36] Nolland, *Luke 9:21–18:34*, 581.

[37] Kee, *Testaments of the Twelve Patriarchs*, 777–78.

[38] See M. de Jonge, *The Testaments of the Twelve Patriarchs: A Study of Their Text, Composition and Origin*, 2nd ed. (Assen: Van Gorcum, 1975); and M. de Jonge, "The Testaments of the Twelve Patriarchs: Central Problems and Essential Viewpoints," in *Aufstieg und Niedergang der römischen Welt*, Part 2, Principat, 20.1, ed. Wolfgang Haase and Hildegard Temporini (Berlin: Walter de Gruyter, 1987): 359–420.

[39] Marinus de Jonge, "'The Testaments of the Twelve Patriarchs' and Related Qumran Fragments," in *For a Later Generation: The Transformation of Tradition in Israel, Early Judaism, and Early Christianity*, ed. Randal A. Argall, Beverly Bow, and Rodney Alan Werline (Harrisburg, PA: Trinity Press International, 2000), 66.

a few others (not Issachar or Dan) are portions of prior Jewish documents on which the present testaments were in part based.[40] While some would disagree with de Jonge, there has not yet been, to my knowledge, an adequate refutation of his argument.

We can conclude, then, that nowhere else is there evidence of the love of God (the Shema)[41] and the love of neighbor (Leviticus 19:18) being used together as a way of reading or summarizing the law. Moreover, we certainly have no evidence of the kind of formulation that we find in Luke 10, particularly in light of the uncertainty surrounding the *Testaments of the Twelve Patriarchs*. While there are no exact parallels, however, we should recognize that what we have in the Synoptics did not arrive out of nowhere. That is, elements in Second Temple Judaism would have paved the way for such a statement. We move, then, to an important connection that was made in the liturgical life of Judaism, which can serve as a bridge from Second Temple Judaism to the material we have in the Synoptics. This connection is the connection between the Shema and the Decalogue.

THE SHEMA, LEVITICUS 19:18, AND THE DECALOGUE

In his article "Mark 12.28–31 and the Decalogue," Dale C. Allison Jr. argues that the Synoptic summary of the law through the double love command would have been commonplace in its historical context because of the Decalogue. He points to *On the Decalogue*, a text we have already examined, to argue that Philo understood the Decalogue as the summary of the whole law, and love of God/love of neighbor as the summary of the Decalogue. He further argues that the Shema was understood to be a summary of the first half, while Leviticus 19:18 was understood to be the summary of the second half. Consequently, readers of the Synoptics would naturally have thought of the Decalogue when they read the double love command.[42] The double love command would have seemed quite normal to those readers.

---

[40] Ibid., 77.

[41] I will use the title "Shema" throughout this paper to describe the command to love God in Deuteronomy 6:5, although, properly understood, the Shema refers to the entirety of Deuteronomy 6:4–9.

[42] Dale C. Allison Jr., "Mark 12.28–31 and the Decalogue," in *The Gospels and the Scriptures of Israel*, ed. Craig A. Evans and William Richard Stegner (Sheffield, England: Sheffield Academic Press, 1994), 273.

Can the Synoptics' double love command be understood as a summary of the Decalogue? A long history associates the Shema with the Decalogue. In Deuteronomy 5–6, the Decalogue and the Shema are paralleled with each other. The reader is expected to associate the Decalogue with the Shema, understanding them as roughly similar, perhaps even as equivalent.[43] The connection between the Shema and the Decalogue is attested by other ancient sources. The Nash Papyrus, a Hebrew papyrus dating from no later than the first century CE,[44] combines the two, perhaps for liturgical purposes.[45] Here, the Shema immediately follows the Decalogue,[46] a juxtaposition that gives credence to the idea that they were understood similarly. Allison also quotes later rabbinic sources, which state that during Second Temple Judaism, the Shema and Decalogue were recited together.[47] The Dead Sea Scrolls also confirm the practice of recitation. Esther Eshel observes that in 4QDeut[n] the Shema and Decalogue are also printed together. Eshel hypothesizes that it may have served as a prayer book. Thus, the Decalogue and the Shema may have been used together as a liturgical device.[48] Nowhere, however, did the Shema need to be accompanied by Leviticus 19:18 or a similar command in order to stand by the Decalogue. It was understood to be adequate on its own.

---

[43] This parallel can be seen in the same basic structure in each of the two major sections. Starting in Deuteronomy 5, we see the order of the call to Israel (Hear, O Israel—v. 1), the teaching of the central ethical principle (the Decalogue—vv. 6–21), a short homily on obedience as a requirement for prosperity (vv. 22–33), and an exhortation on teaching children the principle (6:1–3). Starting in Deuteronomy 6:4–25 we see a similar structure: the call to Israel (Hear, O Israel (v. 4), the teaching of the central ethical principle (vv. 4–5), a short homily on obedience (vv. 10–19), and an exhortation on teaching children (vv. 20–25).

[44] F. C. Burkitt, "The Hebrew Papyrus of the Ten Commandments," *Jewish Quarterly Review* 15 (1903): 407.

[45] Allison, "Mark 12.28–31 and the Decalogue," 275.

[46] The form of the Decalogue may contain elements from both Exodus and Deuteronomy (Burkitt, "The Hebrew Papyrus of the Ten Commandments," 397–99).

[47] Allison, "Mark 12.28–31 and the Decalogue," 275. Allison points specifically to *m. Tamid* 5:1; *b. Ber.* 12a; and *Sipre Deut.* 34.

[48] Esther Eshel, "4QDeut[n]—A Text That Has Undergone Harmonistic Editing," *Hebrew Union College Annual* 62 (1991), ed. Herbert H. Paper (Cincinnati: Hebrew Union College, 1992), 151–52.

Allison is doubtless correct that the connection between the Shema and the Decalogue was well understood. There is less evidence, however, that the Shema was understood as the summary of the first five commandments. In content, the Shema approximates the first commandment most closely. However, in the various settings connecting the Shema and the Decalogue, there seems to be the assumption that the Shema is somewhat equivalent to the Decalogue as a whole. If Allison's hypothesis were correct, we would expect that Leviticus 19:18 or some similar command would be recited after the Shema in Deuteronomy 6 or in a liturgical fragment. We find no evidence of this recitation. In fact, the larger context of Deuteronomy 5–6 focuses solely on loyalty to God.

Indeed, Allison argues that it was common to use the Shema to summarize the first half of the law and to use Leviticus 19:18 to summarize the latter half. We have seen that the former claim cannot be substantiated, although some connection between the Shema and the Decalogue clearly exists. To support the latter claim, Allison appeals to Paul in Romans 13:9 and to Christian materials dating well after the Synoptics.[49] In Romans 13:9, Paul lists four of the Ten Commandments (all from the second half), summarizing them with Leviticus 19:18. But Paul understands Leviticus 19:18 to summarize not only those four particular commandments but "any other commandment" as well. That is, Romans 13:9 can be used to argue for a connection between Leviticus 19:18 and the Decalogue, but it cannot be used to argue for an understanding of Leviticus 19:18 as a summary of only the second half of the Decalogue.[50] Moreover, the connection between Leviticus 19:18 and the Decalogue may be a uniquely Christian one, as no other non-Christian Jewish source can support such a connection. Thus, while there does seem to be a connection between Leviticus 19:18 and the Decalogue in Paul, no evidence supports the view that it was understood to summarize only the second half of the Decalogue.

---

[49] Allison, "Mark 12.28–31 and the Decalogue," 274–75. Clearly, the *Didache* and the writings of the early church fathers cannot be used as evidence for what was natural for Second Temple Judaism when such writings probably drew their ideas specifically from the Synoptics themselves.

[50] Similarly, Luke 18:18–30 quotes not just "second tablet" commandments from the Decalogue but also includes the fifth commandment. It is not at all clear that Luke 18 seeks to summarize *only* the second half of the Decalogue.

In summary, much evidence supports a connection between the Shema and the Decalogue in Second Temple Judaism. The nature of that connection is unclear, but the two seem to have been understood in a similar way. Early New Testament evidence connects Leviticus 19:18 with the Decalogue. Once again, the nature of the connection is unclear, but like the Shema, it seems to have been understood to be similar in essence to the Decalogue as a whole. We begin to see a bridge, then, between the Synoptics and their historical context. The Shema and Leviticus 19:18 were both traditional ways of summarizing the Decalogue. But because only Romans connects Leviticus 19:18 to the Decalogue, this may have been a specifically Christian Jewish bridge.

The uniqueness of Luke's one-command formulation

We began this section with Sanders's argument that what we have in the Synoptics about the double love command is typical of its historical context. But we have been unable to find enough evidence to support this argument. Some material makes it thinkable that the double love command would not have been revolutionary. After all, the notion that piety and justice constitute the chief duties of people, and that the Decalogue does allow for such a summary, would mean that the double love commandment was not radical. The connections between the Shema and the Decalogue, and the Christian Jewish connections between Leviticus 19:18 and the Decalogue, demonstrate how such texts could reasonably have been brought together. I agree with Marshall, who concludes that "the linking of the two commandments may accordingly have taken place in Judaism, but it is doubtful whether we should go further than saying that Judaism had by this time provided an atmosphere in which the combination was natural."[51]

I conclude, then, that this combination found in the Synoptics, while not entirely novel to Second Temple Judaism, was not typical. And Luke's one-command formulation must be understood as much less common. No evidence in Second Temple Judaism combines in one command love of God and love of neighbor as a sole requirement. It is unique, in formulation and implication. With regard to content, the uniqueness of Luke 10:27 will be determined by what we judge to be the significance of the one-command formulation. In light of the evidence,

---

[51] Marshall, *The Gospel of Luke*, 444.

we may rightly understand the one command of Luke 10:27 to be extraordinary and, depending on its ramifications, even groundbreaking.

IS LUKE'S ONE-COMMAND FORMULATION SIGNIFICANT?

I am assuming that the one command in Luke 10:27 is significant; now we explore how that significance should be understood. We have thus far argued that Luke has intentionally crafted the double love command in this new way, in the midst of a narrative that Luke has reworked to better suit the purposes of the Gospel. Furthermore, we have seen that both the pairing of the Shema and Leviticus 19:18 and Luke's singular formulation are unique in their historical context. Thus, we are led to believe that the one command has a significant role to play, both in the particular narrative where Luke has placed it and in Luke's theology.

But two preliminary issues threaten these assumptions. The first asks whether we are dealing with a case of an ellipsis in Luke 10:27, the same question that we raised in the matter of the Testaments of the Twelve Patriarchs. The second issue is an argument from the fact that the one command comes from the mouth of the lawyer, not Jesus. Does the change in speaker imply that even Luke understood this version of the double love command to be commonplace? After addressing these two issues, we will be in a position to examine the significance of the one command in Luke 10:25–37. First, we will investigate the broader literary unit of Luke-Acts to determine what else is said about love of God and love of neighbor. Second, we will explore the central thrust of Luke 10:25–37. Finally, we will argue for the exact nature of the one command's significance.

The possibility of an ellipsis in Luke 10:27

In our evaluation of the *Testaments of the Twelve Patriarchs*, we discounted the presence there of the love of God and neighbor compressed into one command. We did so on the premise that what we had there was an ellipsis, a case where the second verb is implied but not written. One might well wonder if the same criticism could not be leveled against Luke 10:27. This is a difficult question, because the criteria for determining an ellipsis are not established. On what basis can we claim that what we have in the testaments is an ellipsis, but what we have in Luke 10:27 is not?

First, Luke 10:27 consists of two quotations from the OT. We have seen that the material in the testaments was not quotations. It seems to me that in the case of a quotation, one will be more careful to copy word for word. Inversely, any change in wording of a quotation must be considered more significant than a change to a general inherited tradition, especially when the parallels are not so worded. That is to say, an ellipsis is less likely to be used in a quotation than in normal material, assuming, of course, that the material being quoted was not originally formulated with an ellipsis.

Second, context matters. An ellipsis is used primarily for the purpose of conciseness. An author is more likely to use an ellipsis in a long list of commands and exhortations than in two commands standing alone. We observed that all three passages where love of God and love of neighbor were connected in the testaments occurred in the midst of a larger list of commands. We can say, then, that it would be more natural to assume an ellipsis there than in Luke 10:27.

Finally, a particular author's writing patterns matter. Is the ellipsis commonly used by the author in question? In *Testament of Dan* 6:8, we have two occurrences of such a practice. Both occur after an aorist imperative, the form of verb used in 5:3. In fact, in the second of these two occurrences, the verb is ἀγαπήσατε, precisely the same word used in 5:3.[52] Does Luke commonly use such a technique? For Luke, the kind of verb in question is the future indicative. Luke's Gospel includes ten occurrences of the future indicative active, second person singular, the form we find in 10:27. Of those ten, only 10:27 uses the verb to apply to two different objects. There are eleven occurrences of the future indicative active, second person plural. Of those eleven, none is formulated like Luke 10:27. In other words, at no other time does Luke employ an ellipsis when using a second person future indicative verb. The author of the *Testament of Dan* is apparently more likely to use an ellipsis that Luke is. We seem to be justified in calling the testaments' usage an ellipsis but not Luke's. Luke is quoting particular passages, he is not in the midst of a long list of exhortations, and he never formulates any other future indicative clauses in such a way. Luke 10:27 is not an ellipsis; rather, it collapses two commands into one.

---

[52] Charles, *Greek Versions of the Testaments of the Twelve Patriarchs*, 141.

Is the one-command formulation Jesus' or the lawyer's?

Does the text itself imply that what is being said is typical of its historical context? In testing stories, we expect the final answer to come from the mouth of Jesus. Furthermore, we expect his answer to be startling in some way, declaring to the one asking the question something that was not commonplace. In Luke 10:25–27, however, the response is put not in the mouth of Jesus but in the mouth of the lawyer. Does this fact imply that the one command was well known to the lawyers? As we shall see, Luke has clearly transferred the weight of this narrative to the lawyer's second question, "Who is my neighbor?" Does this transfer indicate an assumption on Luke's part that what has come before would be readily accepted by all?

Such reasoning is flawed. First, we have seen that Luke is well aware that the tradition attributed these words to Jesus. Moreover, it was the formulation of the double command itself that was of significance in the tradition. That was the "startling" answer that Jesus gave to the lawyer/scribe. Moreover, Luke's unique formulation suggests a concern for the way the command is understood. It would be odd, then, for Luke to imply that such a reading was commonplace.

The mistake in the posing of the questions above is that it takes a Lukan redaction and asks a question of it that Luke is not trying to answer through his redaction. Luke has redacted the Q and Mark material to parallel the narrative in Luke 18:18–25. In the structure of both narratives, the first answer sets the stage for the more central question and answer. In Luke 18, the list of the commandments sets the stage for addressing the issue of wealth. In Luke 10, the one-command formulation sets the stage for the more central question: "Who is my neighbor?" In both cases, the weight of the narrative falls on Jesus' later answer. Luke has not redacted the material in order to argue that people would readily accept the one love command.

One might still raise the objection that in Luke 10, it is the lawyer who voices the one-command formulation. Does it follow that such an understanding was common among such people? Again, no. The central focus of the narrative must be moved to the second question-and-answer sequence. In order to refocus the narrative, Luke has put Jesus' words (which he knows from Q and Mark) in the lawyer's mouth. This move minimizes their rhetorical effect so that the suspense of the narrative is maintained until the real climax of the story. Thus, Luke has redacted the story for a particular purpose. To argue that the one-command formulation is common because the lawyer articulates it is to misunderstand the author's rhetorical strategy.

Although the shift in focus is the central motivation behind Luke's putting the one command in the mouth of the lawyer, we might surmise a supplemental reason. We might say that at this point Luke is following Mark. While Mark at first records the double love command as coming from the mouth of Jesus, the scribe repeats it (Mark 12:33). We may then understand the lawyer's words as merely Jesus' words which the lawyer is repeating back to him.[53] This proposal makes sense when we consider that Luke knows the tradition of Mark and Q and is redacting it. It also makes sense, in Luke's larger scheme, that the author would place the real emphasis of the narrative on the answer to the question, "Who is my neighbor?" If the lawyer is indeed repeating Jesus' words back to him, then the test the lawyer brings before Jesus is in his second question rather than his first. The entire section of verses 25–27, then, is best understood as a rehearsal for the real testing. The lawyer is asking a question to which he knows Jesus' answer. When Jesus makes him answer it, he simply repeats Jesus' answer. All this is a way to get to the real testing question, "Who is my neighbor?"[54]

There is no reason, then, to conclude that the one command was common knowledge simply because it is articulated by the lawyer in Luke's account. Rather, Luke's placement of the words in the lawyer's mouth gives a new feel to the narrative as a whole. It delays the climax of the narrative until the lawyer's second question and Jesus' answer to that question. This change in focus is exactly what Luke intends. By grasping this insight, we are well on our way to understanding the central thrust of the narrative.

---

[53] A similar idea is put forth by T. W. Manson, who also argues that the lawyer is giving Jesus' answer back to him. But he argues this point not on the basis of a literary dependency on Mark but on the grounds that "great teachers constantly repeat themselves." It would have been natural, then, for the lawyer to be well aware of Jesus' stance on this particular question. See Manson, *The Sayings of Jesus as Recorded in the Gospels according to St. Matthew and St. Luke* (London: SCM Press, 1961), 259–61.

[54] This is also the position of John J. Kilgallen, in "The Plan of the NOMIKOΣ (Luke 10.25–37)," *New Testament Studies* 42 (1996): 615–19.

Loving God and neighbor in Luke-Acts

Before we come to the central focus of Luke 10:25–37, however, we are well advised to explore the theme of love of God and love of neighbor in the broader literary work of Luke. The theme of love of God is not common in the work. The most explicit reference to such love is found in Luke 11:42. Here Jesus criticizes the Pharisees for neglecting justice and the love of God. While we are not given much information about what it means to love God, we note an interesting connection between loving God and justice. Are they understood to be the same thing? A second, more implicit reference is found in Luke 16:13. Here, love of God is an alternative to love of wealth. Third, in Luke 18:18–25, love of wealth is contrasted with the proper interpretation of the Decalogue, which is summarized with commands dealing more with the ethical treatment of other humans. Love of God is a rare topic in Luke, and when it is mentioned, it is not easily distinguishable from love of neighbor.

Love of others is a more prominent theme. Luke 6:27–36 speaks repeatedly of the need for love of enemies in particular. Clearly, love is not to be understood as directed merely toward one's own people, but rather is to be shown to those who will not return one's love.[55] This amazingly explicit command to love enemies is shared with Matthew; it likely stems from the Q tradition. It is at odds to a certain extent with the historical context from which it came. Is there a connection here between love of neighbor and love of God? Luke 6:35 identifies as children of God those who love their enemies. Verse 36 is more explicit: Γίνεσθε οἰκτίρμονες καθὼς [καὶ] ὁ πατὴρ ὑμῶν οἰκτίρμων ἐστίν (Be merciful, just as your Father is merciful). The basis for showing mercy (itself equated with love) is the fact that God shows mercy. In

---

[55] This view contrasts with the typical understandings of Leviticus 19:18 in Second Temple Judaism. Love was commanded toward one's own fellow citizens, and even to the stranger living among them, but not to the enemy. Much of the evidence points to an explicit lack of love for outsiders. Marshall observes the tendency to understand "neighbor" to refer only to fellow Jews, explicitly excluding Samaritans and foreigners (Marshall, *The Gospel of Luke*, 444). One observes hatred of Rome, particularly in light of 70 CE. Qumran documents command believers to love the sons of light but to hate and exclude the sons of darkness (1QS 1:10; 9:21ff). Here, "sons of darkness" refers to those outside community boundaries. "Neighbor," then, continued to be used to refer to fellow citizens or something similar.

the story of the woman who kissed Jesus' feet (Luke 7:36–50), love is connected with forgiveness. It is unclear, however, whether this is love for God or neighbor, or for both.

Those listed above are all the relevant passages in which love is specifically mentioned. The proper treatment of others, however, is a concern for Luke even when the word ἀγαπάω is not explicitly used. Throughout his ministry, as recorded in the Gospel of Luke, Jesus is especially concerned with the oppressed, the poor, and the marginalized—people not held in high regard by society. Jesus shows compassion for Gentiles, women, and outsiders. In Luke 9:51–56, the disciples consider calling destruction down on Samaritans who did not receive them. Jesus' response was to rebuke his disciples. Jesus consistently rejects the option of violence and coercion, commending instead the way of love. Even on the cross, Jesus' cry is for forgiveness, even of those responsible for crucifying him. Love of all human beings, whether they are poor or oppressed, enemies or outsiders, is a central theme of the Gospel of Luke.

The central focus of Luke 10:25–37

In a Gospel that again and again emphasizes love, the narrative of 10:25–37 fits well. We have seen that the tradition has been reworked so that the emphasis no longer falls on love of God and love of neighbor as the fulfillment of the law. Rather, that word is given to the lawyer, in order to transfer the climax of the story answering the question "Who is my neighbor?" We have also seen that this question is the real test for Jesus. For the moment, the lawyer is granting Jesus his summary of the law as love of God and neighbor, in order to force Jesus to define the implications of that summary.[56] What are the proper boundaries regarding who should be the object of one's love?

---

[56] It could be argued that the phrase "wanting to justify himself," before the question "Who is my neighbor?" argues against this reading, because this latter question seems to be an afterthought, born of resentment. But J. Ian H. McDonald, among others, argues that this phrase concerning self-justification "probably suggests a combative ethos rather than resentment." See McDonald, "Rhetorical Issue and Rhetorical Strategy in Luke 10.25–37 and Acts 10.1–11.18," in *Rhetoric and the New Testament: Essays from the 1992 Heidelberg Conference*, ed. Stanley E. Porter and Thomas H. Olbricht (Sheffield, England: Sheffield Academic Press, 1993), 66.

The positioning of the narrative is important as well: the parable of the good Samaritan becomes the real climax of the story. Also, Luke's placing of this narrative in this section of the Gospel is significant. Had he located it after 20:40 (paralleling Matthew's and Mark's placement), the narrative would have served a completely different purpose. There, the issue is authority. Who has it: Jesus or the Jewish leaders/teachers of the law? The narrative in its present location is part of the larger literary section focused on Jesus' journey to Jerusalem. As in all the Synoptics, this section deals primarily with discipleship. That this is the true content of the narrative is evident from the very first question about inheriting eternal life.[57] Readers of texts in this section will naturally ask what this text has to say about what it means to follow Jesus.

The question of how to identify one's neighbor was a live issue in Second Temple Judaism.[58] Scholars have long recognized, however, that in the parable of the good Samaritan, Jesus does not explain who one's neighbor is. The final twist, a twist that we expect in this kind of a narrative, is that the primarily issue is not who is my neighbor but what kind of neighbor I am. This latter formulation places no restriction on the category *neighbor*; no one is excluded from it.[59] Ultimately, defining who my neighbor is, is not the issue. In essence, Jesus told the lawyer, you need to be a neighbor to whoever needs your help. The story itself depicts the most unlikely character—a Samaritan—helping a Jew.[60]

---

[57] Sylvia C. Keesmaat observes that the question is not about getting to heaven but rather about the nature of God's coming kingdom. See Keesmaat, "Strange Neighbors and Risky Care," in *The Challenge of Jesus' Parables*, ed. Richard N. Longenecker (Grand Rapids: Eerdmans, 2000), 276–77. As such, it is more a matter of discipleship than of the eternal state of one's soul.

[58] See above n. 42. Also, Joel B. Green observes that "as a consequence of Hellenistic imperialism and Roman occupation, it could not be generally assumed in the first century of the Common Era that those dwelling among the people of Israel qualified as 'neighbors.'" See Green, *The Gospel of Luke*, New International Commentary on the New Testament, ed. Gordon D. Fee (Grand Rapids: Eerdmans, 1997), 429.

[59] Frederick W. Danker comments, referring also back to Luke 6:31–36, "Divine mercy does not ask the worth of the recipient. It only sees the need. Herein lies the creative possibility for action not measured by rules for neighborly behavior." See Danker, *Jesus and the New Age: A Commentary on the Third Gospel* (St. Louis: Clayton Publishing House, 1972), 133.

[60] The Samaritan is thus set up as an example for Jesus' Jewish audience to follow, an offensive example, to say the least. Robert C. Tannehill characterizes Jesus as "urging

The main point, then, is not how to sum up the law, but what love of God and neighbor really means. Just as in the narrative in Luke 18:18–25, Jesus reinterprets and redefines the meaning of the law. As the laws of the Decalogue called the ruler in Luke 18:18-25 to do much more than he was willing to do—to surrender all other ties of loyalty and allegiance—so the one command of love calls the individual to surrender all prejudice and hatred and to love everyone, without discrimination. In essence, then, the parable of the good Samaritan interprets the command: Love God and neighbor.[61]

The significance of the one command

We are finally in a position to answer the question of the significance of the one-command formulation. While the center of the narrative is the parable of the good Samaritan, the above account makes it clear that the formulation of the one command is significant. The narrative centers on the proper meaning of loving God and neighbor. Because Luke has intentionally formulated the command in this way, we must seek the purpose that this formulation has. What are the implications of making love of God and neighbor a single command? How does collapsing love of God and love of neighbor into one command aid Luke in making the point that is made in the parable of the good Samaritan?

The most obvious and immediate implication of Luke's one command is that love of God and love of neighbor are more closely connected than they would otherwise be. Love of God and love of neighbor are made inseparable. This point is different from saying that both love of God and love of neighbor are central or that together they fulfill the law. It is different from saying that one command is greatest and the other is second. These formulations drive a wedge between the two

---

the religious leaders to move beyond their established limits of concern to include the sinner, the poor, the enemy. Through the parable of the Good Samaritan and the following command (10:37), the lawyer is asked to follow an enemy who ignores such limits and thereby becomes a disturbing example." See Tannehill, *The Narrative Unity of Luke-Acts: A Literary Interpretation*, vol. 1 (Philadelphia: Fortress Press, 1986), 180.

[61] It is not uncommon for commentators to conclude that the parable of the good Samaritan is a kind of commentary on Leviticus 19:18 (see, for example, Green, *The Gospel of Luke*, 425–26). I am suggesting, however, that the parable be understood as a commentary on the entire command: love God and neighbor. Because they are united, the parable should be understood to be "narrative exegesis" (ibid., 426) on both.

commands. Only here are they combined in a way that makes them interdependent. As Joseph Fitzmyer observes, "No love of God is complete without that of one's neighbor."[62] We might say that in order to fulfill the law, one must do both. There is no partial credit for doing one of the two.

Still, this statement does not seem strong enough. In observing the connection the Shema and Leviticus 19:18 have with the Decalogue, we noted that it is not clear that the Shema was understood to summarize the first half and Leviticus 19:18 the second half. Rather, whenever either was used in connection with the Decalogue, the implication was that either summarized the entire Decalogue. In Paul, we find the inference that Leviticus 19:18 is a summary of all commands. That is to say, love of God and love of neighbor are both ways to summarize the whole of what the law requires.

In Luke, love of neighbor takes center stage. While love of God remains a peripheral issue, love of other people is at the heart of Luke's Gospel. Moreover, in Luke 18 and Luke 10, our parallel narratives, the law is interpreted in terms of love of neighbor. Even in Luke 10, where the love of God is mentioned, the good Samaritan parable interprets the meaning of this obligation in conjunction with love of neighbor. The larger implication of this formulation is that loving God and loving neighbor is one action, that in fact we love God precisely by loving our neighbor. We might also add, in light of the various teachings in Luke on love, that we love others because God loves them,[63] and that we are able to love others because God loves—and forgives—us.[64] The two commands are fully intertwined, but the love of neighbor is central: in order to love God, we must love the neighbor.[65] Loving the neighbor fulfills the command to love God, but the love of God also informs what loving the neighbor means (i.e., what being a neighbor is). Apart from

---

[62] Fitzmyer, *The Gospel according to Luke (X–XXIV)*, 878.

[63] Luke 6:36.

[64] Luke 7:36–50.

[65] R. Alan Culpepper comes close to this conclusion (although it is not quite as radical as the one argued in the paper): "There is no dichotomy between the commands to love God and to love one's neighbor. Indeed, when one loves God, one lives out love for others as well (see I John 4:7–21)." See Culpepper, "The Gospel of Luke," *The New Interpreter's Bible*, vol. 9, ed. Leander E. Keck (Nashville: Abingdon Press, 1995), 228.

1 John, the New Testament contains no stronger statement connecting love of God and love of neighbor.

With respect to the broader theme or focus of the narrative in Luke 10:25–37, the formulation of one command serves Luke's larger goals. The formulation enables Luke to reinterpret love of neighbor as love of God. Moreover, in a narrative where the central point is the duty to be a neighbor to those in need, the placement of this obligation at the heart of the law is significant: even love of God is dependent on love of neighbor.[66] The issue of who one's neighbor is becomes much more important when loving the neighbor carries this kind of weight. There is no avoiding it. One must deal with it, because apart from such love, one cannot be faithful to the Torah—no matter how much one claims to love God.

---

[66] This statement needs to be qualified. We have no reason to doubt that for Luke the love of God was of supreme importance, second to nothing. By "dependent," I mean only that it is specifically the love of neighbor by which one performs the all-important task of loving God.

CHAPTER FOUR

The double love command: Matthew's hermeneutical key

Amy Barker

H ow did all three Synoptics come to combine the two love commands from the Torah[1] and ascribe them to Jesus? That question launched the writing of the essays in this collection. Was this combination unique to Jesus? Was it adopted or modified from existing Hellenistic Jewish culture? How does Matthew's redaction compare with its Synoptic parallels, and what might this comparison reveal about the Matthean hermeneutic of Jesus? And what happened to the Shema of Deuteronomy 6:4? Why, when it is cited by Mark the forerunner, do Matthew and Luke omit it?

This chapter examines Matthew's rendering of the double love command in hope of advancing the discussion of these questions. I will follow the order of the text of Matthew 22:34–40 and comment on certain concepts and contextual matters as they arise in the passage. Following these comments, I hope to demonstrate that the double love commandment is foundational to an understanding of Matthew's hermeneutic of Jesus.

PHARISEES AND OTHERS

Οἱ δὲ Φαρισαῖοι ἀκούσαντες ὅτι ἐφίμωσεν τοὺς Σαδδουκαίους συνήχθησαν ἐπὶ τὸ αὐτό.

22:34 But when the Pharisees heard that he had put the Sadducees to silence, they gathered themselves together.[2]

---

[1] Deut. 6:4–5 and Lev. 19:18.

[2] Unless otherwise indicated, translations are mine.

A look at the broader context of Matthew 22:14–45 reveals a series of interrogations by the Pharisees and Sadducees. In verse 15, the Pharisees are named as first interrogators; they "counseled together" in order to trap Jesus in what he said. After their initial question about paying tax to the emperor, the Pharisees "marveled" over Jesus' answer and went away (v. 22). Then the Sadducees posed a second question, about the resurrection (vv. 23–33); Jesus' answer to them astonished the multitudes. Now, in verse 34, the Pharisees have returned to resume the interrogation, having heard that Jesus had "put the Sadducees to silence." They again "gathered themselves together,"[3] in a way suggesting a continuation of the plot against Jesus noted in verse 15.[4]

Matthew's negative and monolithic treatment of the Pharisees does not accord well with current scholarship that posits a nuanced understanding of the Pharisees as closer to Jesus than earlier scholars imagined.[5] However, although James Dunn argues that there were more similarities than differences between Jesus and the Pharisees, he does not deny the conflict between them. Rather, he argues that depicting Jesus as "very close to the Pharisees, not least on matters of the law, is

---

[3] Matthew uses συνάγω (to gather) twenty-four times.

[4] Daniel Patte, *The Gospel according to Matthew: A Structural Commentary on Matthew's Faith* (Philadelphia: Fortress Press, 1987), 313.

[5] Current scholarship provides an abundance of material that corrects prejudicial views about the Pharisees in the first century. E. P. Sanders (*Jesus and Judaism* [Philadelphia: Fortress Press, 1985]); James Dunn, and others work to mitigate the polemical tendencies against the Pharisees in Matthew. Philip Sigal distinguishes the *Pharisaioi* from the *perushim,* who (although their identity remains unclear) were a group of pietistic sectarian Jews from various circles within Judaism. Sigal makes this distinction in order to point to the *perushim* as the objects of Jesus' condemnation. He places Jesus within proto-rabbinic Judaism, not in discord with the Pharisees. Viewed in this light, Jesus applied halakic principles with freedom of interpretation and with authority, in conformity with proto-rabbinic Judaism. See Phillip Sigal, *The Halakah of Jesus of Nazareth according to the Gospel of Matthew* (Lanham, MD: University Press of America, 1986), 9. James Dunn finds it unnecessary to determine the precise relation between the *haberim* or *perushim* and the Pharisees. "That there were at the time of Jesus a number of Pharisees, and probably a significant body of Pharisees, who felt passionately concerned to preserve, maintain, and defend Israel's status as the people of the covenant and the righteousness of the law, as understood in the already developed halakoth, must be regarded as virtually certain" (James D. G. Dunn, "Pharisees, Sinners, and Jesus," in *The Social World of Formative Christianity and Judaism,* ed. Jacob Neusner [Philadelphia: Fortress Press, 1988], 274).

to *increase* the likelihood of tension between Jesus and the Pharisees, not to lessen it. . . . A successful Jesus who was observant of the law and yet not a Pharisee or *haber* was bound to be regarded as some sort of competitor and to cause some friction and conflict."[6]

Nonetheless, it is difficult to disregard Matthew's negative casting of Jewish leaders as antagonists of Jesus. "Matthew looks upon the representatives of Israel as a homogeneous group. The many names he eventually gives the Jewish leaders are not meant as further historical information. He does not want to introduce a distinction between Pharisees, Sadducees, scribes, high priests and elders. In his eyes they are all equally representatives of the one Israel."[7]

Viewing the larger context of Matthew 22:15–46, Matthew's amalgamation of the various parties into one homogeneous antagonistic group is manifest in his introduction to each of the four questions. The Pharisees are introduced as the first subject, beginning in verse 15. The Herodians join the Pharisees in their plot against Jesus (v. 16), as do the Sadducees (v. 23). The Pharisees, represented by a νομικός (lawyer), are the stated antagonists in verses 34–35; they are named again in verse 41. Matthew intentionally places the Pharisees in conflict with Jesus as "prototypical antagonists of Jesus in Matthew."[8] This antagonism became evident in Matthew 21, in Jesus' telling of the parable of the vineyard; the Pharisees knew that Jesus was indicting them (Matt. 21:45).

Patte's reading of the Pharisees in Matthew 22 unites them with the Sadducees. In his discussion about Roman tax (Matt. 22:15–22), he describes the Pharisees as unable to distinguish between what would honor God and what would deny God's authority. "This is so because they viewed the 'way of God' as an abstraction totally removed from human affairs."[9] This view unites them with the Sadducees who deny the role of God's power in human affairs (22:23–28). Hence, Matthew can present the two groups as united. Both acknowledge the authority

[6] Dunn, "Pharisees, Sinners, and Jesus," 276.

[7] Sjef van Tilborg, *The Jewish Leaders in Matthew* (Leiden: Brill, 1972), 1.

[8] Raymond F. Collins, "Matthew's *ENTOLAI:* Towards an Understanding of the Commandments in the First Gospel," in *The Four Gospels,* ed. Frans van Segbroeck (Louvain, Belgium: Leuven University Press, 1992), 1338.

[9] Patte, *Matthew,* 314.

of the law over human affairs, calling it "the way of God," even the way to have a good life. But Patte characterizes their view as one in which the law expresses what humans can do for themselves, which implicitly denies the power of God. At the same time, both groups view the authority of the law as being so great, so divine, that it cannot be subject to any human interpretation that might exhibit consideration for people, that might allow flexible interpretation in concrete situations (as Jesus did). In their view, although people must execute God's way in human affairs, human affairs cannot in any way affect God's way; it remains immutable and impermeable. Thus, humans are left with the law as the way of God that humans alone can do. But as will become evident, Jesus offers the dual love command to bridge and join the separation between the divine and human realms presumed by the Pharisees and Sadducees.

An outline of the rest of this pericope highlights what we can anticipate in the dialogue between Jesus and his interrogators.

The questioner asked which (one) commandment.	Jesus replied with *two*.
The questioner asked which one commandment is the *greatest*.	Jesus proffered one as the greatest, adding that it is the *first*—then added that there is also a *second* which is like the first.
The questioner asked about a commandment related to the law.	Jesus related two commandments to the *law and the prophets*.
The questioner asked which commandment is the greatest *in the law*.	Jesus declared that all the law and the prophets hang *on* these two commandments.

TESTING BY AN EXPERT IN THE LAW

καὶ ἐπηρώτησεν εἷς ἐξ αὐτῶν [νομικὸς] πειράζων αὐτόν,	22:35 And one of them, a lawyer, asked him, testing him . . .

Jesus, addressed as teacher, was asked a question by a representative of the Pharisees, an expert in the law, for the purpose of testing him. This interrogator—νομικος[10]—is better referred to as "an expert in the law" (because today's term *lawyer* connotes more than this). Referred to as "one of them," that is, as one of the Pharisees, he is the spokesman for the Pharisees. The three descriptive qualifiers concerning him intensify our focus on him. The third qualification is placed in the climactic position,[11] highlighting his role as tester. Clearly he serves as a foil within the Matthean narrative; he passes from the scene without further mention. By comparing Matthew 4:1, 3 with Matthew 16:1, 19:3, and 22:18, we see that the Pharisees share this testing role with Satan.[12]

Understanding this passage in light of the honor and shame culture of the first century[13] sheds light on the meaning of πειράζω (to

---

[10] "In Josephus, *Nomikos* is used as a proper name; one Josedros son of Nomikos is mentioned. *Nomikos* is also explained as being a Sadducean lawyer. Abrahams suggests that he might have been a Gentile lawyer who had recently become a proselyte or contemplated becoming one, and that this formulation of a question of what is the greatest commandment was derived from a catechismal formula" (Samuel Tobias Lachs, *A Rabbinic Commentary on the New Testament: The Gospels of Matthew, Mark, and Luke* [Hoboken, NJ: KTAV Publishing House, 1987], 280).

[11] The grammatical result is that αὐτόν (him), the object of ἐπηρώτησεν (he asked) in Mark 12:28, becomes the object of πειράζων (testing) in Matt. 22:35.

[12] Collins, "Matthew's *ENTOLAI*," 1339.

[13] "It is becoming an accepted fact that honor and shame were pivotal values in antiquity that structured the daily lives of peoples around the Mediterranean, including Jesus and his disciples" (Jerome H. Neyrey, *Honor and Shame in the Gospel of Matthew* [Louisville, KY: Westminster John Knox Press, 1998], 4). Neyrey suggests that, given that Matthew writes so well, he must have gone to school to learn to write Greek. Matthew was probably trained in the conventional educational manner of the *progymnasmata*, where he learned the genres of praise and blame from rhetorical handbooks.

The Latin word for honor means "glory, respect." The Hebrew word for glory translates as "honor" in the LXX. Thus, in biblical times, honor and glory referred to the same thing: how one was regarded and evaluated socially. Honor could be ascribed through birth or acquired through achieved virtue. The latter was most commonly demonstrated through victories skillfully won in the contest of challenge and riposte. Challenges to one's honor could be positive or negative. Receiving gifts or compliments was regarded as a positive challenge, requiring either reciprocation, or refusal to receive or accept the honor (as when Jesus refused to be called good in Matt. 19:17). Negative challenges were hostile, composed of insults, threats, slanderous accusations, and questions designed to entrap and indict. Bruce J. Malina and Richard L. Rohrbaugh, *Social Science Commentary on the Synoptic Gospels* (Minneapolis: Fortress Press, 1992), 76–77.

test). Used as well for Jesus' testings by the devil in Matthew 4:1, πειράζω does not imply the sort of temptation to which those who are morally weak and who lack self-restraint will succumb. Rather, true to encomium form,[14] Matthew lifts up Jesus as the hero who must be challenged and tested. This is the meaning and implication of πειράζω here. Although Matthew is not unique in casting the Jewish leaders as those who tested Jesus, Matthew highlights this role more than the other Synoptic writers do.[15]

THE QUESTION IN CONTEXT

Διδάσκαλε, ποία ἐντολὴ μεγάλη ἐν τῷ νόμῳ;	22:36	"Teacher, which is the great commandment in the law?"

Before examining the specifics of this question, it is helpful to view this question in its context—the broader context of Matthew 22:15–46, in which there are four challenge-riposte exchanges between Jesus and hostile Jewish leaders. Again, bearing the trademarks of an encomium, Matthew's Gospel portrays Jesus as one who triumphs in these exchanges, proving himself to be the superior interpreter of Torah and scripture.[16]

Challenge-riposte exchanges

Typically there are four steps in a challenge-riposte exchange: (1) claim to honor, (2) challenge to that claim, (3) riposte to the challenge, and (4) public verdict by onlookers. Narratives may not always record all four stages. For example, the claim to honor is often presumed: Jesus'

---

[14] While the Gospel according to Matthew is not a true encomium (a biography form intent on praising its subject), it is clearly modeled after this ancient genre of *bios* in which "an author recounted the deeds and words of a great figure with much the same end as the encomium proper, namely the promotion of central cultural values" (David A. deSilva, *The Hope of Glory: Honor Discourse and New Testament Interpretation* [Collegeville, MN: The Liturgical Press, 1999], 39). See also Neyrey, *Honor and Shame*, 1–2.

[15] Birger Gerhardsson, "The Hermeneutic Program in Matthew 22:37–40," in *Jews, Greeks and Christians: Religious Cultures in Late Antiquity*, ed. Robert Hamerton-Kelly (Leiden: Brill, 1976), 134. Cf. Matt. 16:1; 19:3; 22:18; and 22:35, with the parallels.

[16] Jesus triumphs over several challenges to his authority and person by riposting with a lesson in a closer reading of scripture: Matt. 21:15–17; 21:33–46; 22:23–33; 22:41–46. Significantly, all four of these lessons occur in the climactic chapters of Matthew 21–23, and the last two are in our greater pericope.

honor is the premise of Matthew's Gospel. And sometimes the public response is not noted, although we can assume its existence because, in the world of Jesus and Matthew, all significant social intercourse took place in some public arena.[17] However, the middle steps, the challenge and riposte, are always clearly in view, because they demonstrate what, for the narrator, is the heart of the matter.

This understanding sheds light on the greater pericope of Matthew 22:15–46. Verse 15 introduces the hostile intention of the Pharisees, even their goal of defaming Jesus' honor by trapping him in his words. Then follows the first question, about taxes; Jesus' reply; and the conclusion that the Pharisees, their disciples, and the Herodians "marveled and went away" (v. 22). In the second exchange, the Sadducees question Jesus on the resurrection. At the conclusion of this conversation, the multitudes "were astonished at his teaching" (v. 33). In the third exchange (our pericope), the Pharisees gather themselves together (again) to test Jesus—a challenge to Jesus' honor. The question is posed and Jesus answers, but no response is recorded. But this lack of response only quickens the tempo of the exchange, which concludes when Jesus presses the Pharisees with his own question about the Messiah. Tellingly, the broader pericope closes with this observation: "No one was able to answer him a word, nor did anyone dare from that day on to ask him another question" (v. 46). This conclusion may summarize the response of the Pharisees and crowd to the last two exchanges. The effect of all four controversy dialogues, one piling on top of the other, is compelling. The verdict could hardly be clearer: a din of applause lauds Jesus with honor, an emphatic silence implicates the Jewish leaders with shame.

Talmudic pattern of four questions

Mining the Gospel of Matthew rewards us with a richer understanding of what was at stake for Matthew and his readers. We come to realize how masterfully Matthew holds together the traditional Jewish culture with the pervasive Hellenistic culture, the root of Hebrew faith with the branch of the new church. We see this blending of cultures in this pericope. For even as Matthew uses the tools of Hellenistic honor/shame genre, such as challenge-riposte and encomium, to praise Jesus

---

[17] Neyrey, *Honor and Shame*, 44.

in the language and style of that day, he also deftly employs a Jewish pattern of questioning[18] that is unmistakable in this pericope.

"Our Rabbis taught: Twelve questions did the Alexandrians address to R. Joshua b. Hananiah: Three were of a scientific nature, three were matters of *aggada,* three were nonsense and three were matters of conduct" (*b. Niddah* 69b–70a). These four types of questions can be more adequately distinguished as: (1) questions of a "scientific nature": halachic questions about the application of laws to specific situations; (2) questions of *aggada:* supposed contradictions in the non-halachic parts of scripture; (3) "nonsense" questions: attempts to ridicule a scholar and his interpretations of the scriptures; and (4) questions about "matters of conduct"; questions that deal with theoretical principles in the Torah, that is, issues larger than questions of a "scientific nature." These four types of questions, which provide an adequate test of a rabbi's acumen, are all hostile challenges that seek to "entangle him in his talk" (22:15); they are hardly neutral requests for information.[19]

When we apply this schema of four questions to Matthew 22:15–46, we realize a remarkable fit. (1) The Pharisees ask a "scientific" question of Jesus: "Is it lawful to pay taxes to Caesar or not?" (22:15–22). (2) The Sadducees ask a "nonsense" question about levirate marriage and the resurrection (22:23–33). (3) A lawyer asks about "principles of behavior": "Which is the great commandment in the law?" (22:34–40). And (4) Jesus himself asks the Pharisees the "aggadic" question: "What do you think of the Christ? Whose son is he?" (22:41–46).[20]

---

[18] Its earlier existence need not be ruled out, although we find it documented later in the Talmud.

[19] Neyrey, *Honor and Shame,* 45–46.

[20] Ibid., 47–48.

The conflict milieu

Understanding the significance of conflict[21] provides further illumination of our passage. Significantly, Matthew redacts Mark's pericope by changing the tone of Jesus' exchange with his questioner into one of conflict. In the Markan parallel, the inquirer is open-minded as he and Jesus enjoy a mutually affirming exchange. But Matthew presents a hostile Pharisee who questions Jesus about the great commandment in order to test Jesus. This change in tone suggests that Matthew regarded the correct interpretation of the law as "a major bone of contention between his own community and the leadership of formative Judaism."[22]

One important feature of a conflict story that bears on our pericope is the *chria*, the "short pointed saying" or aphorism, that teaches the significant point.[23] As the final answer to the question or challenge posed, the *chria* is the culmination of the controversy. Rudolf Bultmann calls this the "productive power of the controversy dialogue."[24]

---

[21] Arland J. Hultgren devotes an entire book to examining the effect of conflict stories in the Synoptics (*Jesus and His Adversaries, The Form and Function of the Conflict Stories in the Synoptic Tradition* [Minneapolis: Augsburg Publishing House, 1979]). He suggests that while it is useful to note the Hellenistic forms and genres present in the Synoptics (e.g., encomium and honor/shame in Matthew), these comparative studies must not obscure the particular genre and various *Sitze im Leben* of the conflict stories themselves (19). In other words, conflict stories have features peculiar to themselves that should not be subdued by social science paradigms. And, as we have already noted, conflict settings are not the exclusive domain of Hellenism. Rabbinic tradition would be emasculated if its characteristically controversial conflict dialogues are unacknowledged.

[22] David C. Sim, *The Gospel of Matthew and Christian Judaism: The History and Social Setting of the Matthean Community* (Edinburgh: T&T Clark, 1998), 128. See also Gerhard Barth, "Matthew's Understanding of the Law," in *Tradition and Interpretation in Matthew,* ed. Gunther Bornkamm, Gerhard Barth, Heinz Joachim Held (Philadelphia: Westminster Press, 1963), 85; J. Andrew Overman, *Matthew's Gospel and Formative Judaism: The Social World of the Matthean Community* (Minneapolis: Fortress Press, 1990), 84–85; Hultgren, *Jesus and His Adversaries,* 186; and Rudolf Bultmann, *The History of the Synoptic Tradition* (Peabody, MA: Hendrickson Publishers, 1963), 39–54.

[23] Hultgren, *Jesus and His Adversaries,* 33–34.

[24] Bultmann, *Synoptic Tradition,* 51. Interestingly, he notes "the increasing tendency of the Church to clothe its dominical sayings, its views and its fundamental beliefs in the form of the controversy dialogue" (ibid.).

Matthew's polemic between Jesus and the Pharisees does indeed highlight Jesus' teachings. Jesus' emphasis on love as the hermeneutic for all the law and the prophets becomes striking as a result of its accentuation by conflict. Furthermore, "what is most characteristic about the conflict stories in Matthew is that they portray Jesus as the interpreter of the law for the church,"[25] which supports an even broader objective of Matthew.[26]

THE CHALLENGE TO JESUS' AUTHORITY

Διδάσκαλε, ποία ἐντολὴ μεγάλη ἐν τῷ νόμῳ;	22:36	"Teacher, which is the great commandment in the law?"

Jesus' authority as a teacher is pointedly tested. It is as διδάσκαλος (teacher) that Jesus is addressed by the νομικός. Ironically, although Matthew focuses on Jesus as teacher and on the content of Jesus' teachings, Jesus' disciples never call him teacher, master, or rabbi in Mat-

---

[25] Hultgren, *Jesus and His Adversaries*, 187.

[26] Robert C. Tannehill's literary analysis complements this point (*The Sword of His Mouth* [Minneapolis: Fortress Press, 1975]). Many of the stories that describe Jesus' encounter with others "contain dramatic tension, presenting conflict between persons and a surprising development in a vivid scene" (54). These stories are carefully formed to heighten tension, using forceful and imaginative language in order to shock and to challenge our structured world. "New structure can arise only by attacking the old. Everything important to us has its place within our personal world, and the structures of this world are the means by which we interpret experience. We unconsciously fit whatever we experience into these structures, so experience does not ordinarily challenge them. These interpretive structures have a ravenous appetite, seeking to digest all that we encounter. If speech is to induce 'imaginative shock,' effectively challenging the old structures and suggesting new visions, it must resist such digestion. It must stick in the throat. Forceful and imaginative language can do its work only if it does not fit into our ordinary interpretive structures. The result is tension, which often finds its formal reflection with a text. This helps us to understand the frequent use of antithesis in the Gospels. In antithesis the prevailing perspective is allowed expression so that it can be challenged, and the new perspective appears over against it. Thus the hearer is prevented from subsuming the new perspective under the old. It is this clash of perspectives which is revelatory. . . . The tension of the saying carries with it a demand for decision, a decision in which the hearer has much at stake. The text seeks to block the well-marked path along which the hearer is moving so that it may point to another one—a faint trace leading into an uncharted wilderness. The hearer must decide. Thus the tension in the text awakens an answering tension in the hearer, the tension of having to make a decision" (54).

thew; only Judas addresses him as "Rabbi"—in the context of his betrayal of Jesus (Matt. 26:25, 49). Only outsiders call Jesus "Teacher" in Matthew's narrative.[27] Jesus refers to himself in this way three times (10:24, 25; 26:18), but, again, only in reference to how outsiders know him.[28] Perhaps it is Matthew's view that real disciples know Jesus as much more than teacher, master, or rabbi.

The authority of Jesus' teaching is a principal theme in this section of Matthew. In the previous section (21:18–22:14), Matthew depicted Jesus as the Son of David whose power and authority is derived from God alone. Now, in 22:15–46, Matthew underscores this view, for the authority of Jesus' teaching silences all his Jewish opponents—Herodians, Sadducees, and Pharisees.[29]

The νομικός asks Jesus to name the great (μεγάλη) commandment in the law. Matthew has retained Mark's ποία ἐντολή (which commandment), omitted the copulative, and replaced πρώτη πάντων (first of all) with μεγάλη ἐν ἐν τῷ νόμῳ (great in the law), a Greek expression whose μεγάλη (great) may reflect a Semitic superlative (greatest).[30] With this change, Matthew has altered the parameters and focus of the discussion. Matthew's Jesus is challenged to make a statement about hierarchy among the commandments of the law. What is at stake is "whether Jesus accepts all the statutes of the Torah as of equal importance."[31]

---

[27] Matthew 8:19; 9:11; 12:38; 17:24; 19:16; 22:16, 24, 36.

[28] Anthony J. Saldarini, *Matthew's Christian-Jewish Community* (Chicago: University of Chicago Press, 1994), 96.

[29] Patte, *Matthew*, 308. Saldarini (ibid.) takes up the question of whether Matthew's group might have had anything in common with either Greek or Jewish schools of that day. As we have noted, this Gospel is characterized by a thorough blending of both traditions such that, while the influence of both are evident, it is difficult to decipher when one or the other is operative exclusive of the other. This difficulty is also apparent when we try to determine whether Jesus' disciples were schooled according to a Greek or Jewish model. The role of teachers in both cultures was prominent, their authority extending even to the instruction of rulers; teachers were expected to both teach and confront, and were regarded as sages. Thus, Patte's reading of this text as being primarily an issue of Jesus' teaching authority follows suit.

[30] Collins, "Matthew's *ENTOLAI*," 1340.

[31] Reginald H. Fuller, "The Double Commandment of Love: A Test Case for the Criteria of Authenticity," in *Essays on the Love Commandment*, ed. Luise Schottroff, trans. Reginald H. Fuller and Ilse Fuller (Philadelphia: Fortress Press, 1978), 32.

Such questions were not without precedent in Jewish discussions. Apparently, it was within good proto-rabbinic tradition to discuss, and even argue about, which of the 613 commandments might be regarded as all-inclusive, summary precepts. Rabbi Simlai (third century AD) most fully explained this tradition. He said all 613 commandments could be contained, according to David, in eleven (Psalm 16); according to Isaiah (33:15), in six; according to Micah (6:8), in three (to do justice, love mercy, and walk humbly with God); again according to Isaiah (56:1) in two (to observe justice and do righteousness); and according to Amos 5:4, in one (seek me and live).[32] This penchant for summarizing the commandments was strong in the first century as well.[33]

Unfortunately, translations and commentators have exercised flexibility in translating μεγάλη as either "great" or its superlative "greatest." That its correct translation is "great" is no small point. The form used in the question is μεγάλη, the nominative singular feminine form of μέγας, meaning "great." This form is neither the comparative μείζων nor the superlative μεγίστος (as in 2 Pet. 1:4).[34] Although this question is couched as a test, the Pharisees probably did not imagine that Jesus would place one commandment over another. We have noted that it was common Jewish practice to discern from the

---

[32] Geza Vermes, *Jesus and the World of Judaism* (Philadelphia: Fortress Press, 1983), 45; quoting from *b. Mak.* 24a.

[33] Philo maintained that the Decalogue symbolized all the "special laws" of the Torah. (Philo, *Spec. Laws* 1.1). When asked what one must do to inherit eternal life, Jesus recites from the second half of the Decalogue: "Do not kill! Do not commit adultery! Do not steal! . . . (Mark 10:19). Note that only the parallel passage in Matthew (19:19) concludes with "You shall love your neighbor as yourself" (the last in a list usually signifying the one most important). Hillel, perhaps alive when Jesus was born, summarized the Torah in the golden rule. "What is hateful to you, do not do it to your neighbor. This is the whole Torah; all the rest is only interpretation" (*b. Šabb.* 31a). Jesus cites the golden rule in its positive formulation in the Sermon on the Mount, adding "for this is the law and the prophets" in Matt. 7:12, one of three mentions of this weighty phrase in Matthew (also in Matt. 5:17 and 22:40, our passage). We can conclude that Jesus' reply with the double love command was neither out of line nor unprecedented. What was unprecedented and radical was *how* he characterized these two commands in relation to the law—to the law and the prophets, that is.

[34] W. Grundmann, μέγας, μεγάλη, μέγα in *Greek-English Lexicon of the New Testament and Other Early Christian Literature* [BAGD], 2nd ed., ed. W. Bauer, W. F. Arndt, F. W. Gingrich, F. W. Danker (Chicago: University of Chicago Press, 1979), 497–98.

law what were summarizing principles and commands, so Jesus' double love command response was not all that startling. Judaism already had a strong tradition of summarizing the law in the one command of loving neighbor.[35]

Given that the topic of the law was of vital importance to the Pharisees, it is understandable that one of their questions in Matthew 22 deals with the law. The νομίκος does not ask what rule is most important for *life*; he reflects his own discipline when he asks what is the great commandment of the *law* (ἐν τῷ νόμῳ).[36] To the Jews, the Torah (instruction), or law, referred to a whole complex of symbols and commitments: the Hebrew scriptures, the will of God revealed in the scriptures, the interpretation of those scriptures, even the whole Jewish way of life.[37] A question about the great, or summary, commandment in the Torah forces the respondent to confess his interpretive summary of the whole Torah, to reveal its symbolic center.

INTERPRETIVE CENTER

ὁ δὲ ἔφη αὐτῷ,	22:37	He said to him,
Ἀγαπήσεις κύριον		"'You shall love the Lord

---

[35] This tradition is evident in many places. The earlier citation of Hillel's golden rule is but one. Paul's summary of the law as love of neighbor in Rom. 13:8–10 and Gal. 5:14 is another. It was common Jewish practice to discern the light from the heavy commandments in order to determine the weightier matters of the law. Jesus shows himself adept at this discernment in Matt. 23:23: "For you tithe mint and dill and cumin, and have neglected the weightier provisions of the law: justice and mercy and faithfulness." Rabbis were commonly of the opinion that the light commandments should be observed just as faithfully as the heavy ones, because these too had been commanded by God in the law of Moses (Sim, *Matthew*, 132; E. P. Sanders, *Paul and Palestinian Judaism: A Comparison of Patterns of Religion* [Philadelphia: Fortress Press, 1977], 119–20; Barth, "Matthew's Understanding," 77–78, gives the fullest treatment to the rabbinical tradition).

Matthew's Jesus says as much in Matt. 5:18, declaring that not one jot or tittle of the law will pass away until all is accomplished, and that even the least of the Mosaic commandments must be observed and taught to others (5:19). Thus was it understood that the raising of one commandment over another for the purpose of providing fundamental summary did not, by any means, imply that all the commandments were not of equal importance (Barth, "Matthew's Understanding," 77–78).

[36] Gerhardsson, "Hermeneutic Program," 134.

[37] Anthony J. Saldarini, *Matthew's Christian-Jewish Community*, 57.

τὸν θεόν σου

ἐν ὅλῃ τῇ καρδίᾳ σου

καὶ ἐν ὅλῃ τῇ ψυχῇ σου

καὶ ἐν ὅλῃ τῇ διανοίᾳ σου

your God

with all your heart,

and with all your soul,

and with all your mind.'"

Love command without the Shema

Jesus answered this question with the well-known command of Deuter-onomy 6:5: "You shall love the Lord your God . . ." But why did he omit the all-important Shema of Deuteronomy 6:4 that traditionally accom-panied verse 5? And why is the Shema recited only in Mark (12:29) and not in Matthew 22:37 or Luke 10:27?

A simple response is that Jesus is answering a direct question. He is neither opening a prayer nor beginning liturgical worship; he is neither reading scripture nor delivering a message in the temple or synagogue. Such were the contexts in which the Shema[38] was routinely recited. Presumably, Jesus and the other Jews with him recited the Shema twice daily during morning and evening prayers, according to custom.[39] The Shema was integral to the thought and worship life of the Jewish peo-ple. So perhaps Matthew and Luke omitted it because something so established hardly needed repeating.[40]

Love as command

The future active indicative of ἀγαπάω is used here and in the next verse as a present active imperative, following the form in the LXX: "you shall love." How can love for God be commanded? Can we obey

---

[38] I refer to the Shema primarily in its strictest sense of Deut. 6:4-5, although the exam-ples I cite often include more passages. See chapter one of this book, Jackie A. Wyse, "Loving God as an Act of Obedience: The Shema in Context."

[39] The Nash Papyrus provides early evidence that the Shema was associated with the Decalogue; this combination is found in phylacteries worn by those in the Qumran community. Josephus noted that the Jewish people recited the Shema before making their offerings in the temple, and before any public reading of the law. See Shaye J. D. Cohen, "The Temple and the Synagogue," in *The Cambridge History of Judaism*, ed. William Horbury, W. D. Davies, and John Sturdy (Cambridge: Cambridge University Press, 1999), 304; and William Harbury, "Women in the Synagogue," in *The Cambridge History of Juda-ism*, 366.

[40] Our ongoing challenge as we work to understand texts of the first century is to de-termine the "implicits" that were so prevalent they required no explicit mention, not even in the writings of the New Testament.

the command to love God in the same way that we obey the command not to steal or covet? While the Shema (including both Deut. 6:4 *and* 6:5) was recited alongside the Decalogue, this command to love God was not one of the Ten Commandments.[41] In some sense, then, love for God was not regarded as a command with significance equal to that of the Ten Commandments.

Nevertheless, love is the object of ἐντολή (commandment; LXX and Synoptics). "It is not merely urged upon man; God obliges him to it no less than to the social and cultic laws—in fact more so, for love is conceived as the source of obedience to all other law.... The Deuteronomist presents the great fundamental attitudes of love and reverential fear as the response which man owes to the saving love and power of God the Lord (Deut. 6)."[42]

While it is true that love cannot be mandated in that it must be given freely from one's own heart, yet there are exterior acts, such as faithfulness, truthfulness, generosity, devotion, that provide evidence of the heart's choice to love. While we can imagine some degree of obedience possible in these exterior acts, nonetheless they all depend, if genuine, on an authentic love that characterizes a person's entire being. So it is not the command to love God that somehow "awakens" love. Rather, "love is awakened by the experience of being loved."[43] For this reason, Deuteronomy dwells on the intensity and generosity of God's love for Israel.

The very fact that such love is commanded informs us that the term "commandment" must be given greater breadth and fluidity than we normally ascribe to it. Yet it seems impossible for us not to associate the term "commandment" with its juridical implications. Hence, Matthew O'Connell has coined "the imperative of love" as his preferred way of indicating the biblical "command" to love.

O'Connell's analysis aids our own understanding of this passage. All of God's gifts of life and election and covenant for Israel are present

---

[41] According to Jeanette Krabill, missionary in Ivory Coast for twenty years, African Christians welcomed the Ten Commandments, because these commands helped them know how to live as Christians. And to these ten they added an "eleventh" command: You shall love the Lord your God with all your heart ..."

[42] Matthew J. O'Connell, "The Concept of Commandment in the Old Testament," *Theological Studies* 21 (1960): 362, 376.

[43] O'Connell, "The Concept of Commandment," 376.

and tangible in the term ἐντολή, requiring Israel's wholehearted response. Including love as the foundational aspect of humanity's imperative makes the gift all the more valuable. It reveals that, at the heart of God's relation to humanity, God desires intimate communion with humankind, which in itself provides the strongest reassurance to humanity's fears of God's rejection. At the same time, this imperative of love calls for the greatest sobriety from humans, as we must realize that the will of God can only be carried out by humans if our obedience is wedded with a love for God who first loved us.

Moreover, the imperative of love is intended as law carried into the heart with transformative, redemptive force. Broadening the idea of commandment and law into its fullest canonical sense, God's law represents God's saving action toward and redemption of Israel, and that of the whole world through Israel. However, it is not the law itself that can effect any kind of holiness; no norm or action can do that, not even the new ἐντολή of John. Israel's history clearly demonstrates that the law alone could not overcome the hardness of humanity's heart. Only the law of love, the law of the Spirit, can do that.[44]

Heart, soul, and mind: Matthew's three tones

"Among the Synoptics, only Matthew lists three faculties—heart, soul, and mind. Mark and Luke list four; they both add 'strength,' and reverse the order of the third and fourth faculties."[45] Matthew lists three faculties with which we are to love God just as Deuteronomy lists three. But the third listed in Deuteronomy is strength or power (δύναμις in the LXX), while Matthew lists mind (διανοία)."[46] The Hebrew text of

---

[44] Rom 13:10; 8:2.

[45] Collins, "Matthew's ENTOLAI," 1341.

[46] And Matthew changed Mark's ἐκ to ἐν in order to translate more closely the Hebrew ‫ב‬. Apparently, Matthew used a combination of both Markan and non-Markan material; clearly he used the Masoretic text. A comparison of Matthew with Mark in this pericope and its broader context allows us to see Matthew's use of Mark. The differences that stand out tend to be Semitisms. See Fuller, "The Double Commandment of Love." "Matthew . . . shows such close adherence to the Hebrew, against the LXX, that it is hard to resist the conclusion that he knew and drew on a text very close to our MT. We cannot avoid the possibility that he was following a Targum very close to our Hebrew, but the only wisdom we can have is to follow the evidence we possess, and this leads inevitably to the conclusion that Matthew was master of the Hebrew" (M. D. Goulder, Midrash and Lection in Matthew [London: SPCK, 1974], 125). For example, "he translates

the Shema gives three "tones": to love Yahweh your God with all your heart (לבב) and with all your soul (נפש) and with all your substance (מאד).[47]

Given the Jewish orientation of Matthew's Gospel, and Matthew's predilection to use Semitisms and an abundance of quotations from the Hebrew Bible, we can easily imagine that Matthew quoted Deuteronomy 6:5 according to a first-century Jewish pattern of interpretation based on the Shema. Although some NT scholars are inclined to interpret the three faculties as being symbolic expressions for completeness, not intended to be plumbed for nuanced meanings,[48] there is every evidence that Matthew did intend a full Jewish treatment of these three tones.

But if such be the case, how do we explain Matthew's use of διανοία as a translation for the Hebrew מאד? This Hebrew word allows some breadth of meaning, connoting both might and wealth (*mammon*). The latter meaning seemed to predominate in rabbinic writings, referring to one's property and possessions, which things implied that one had power or strength or might. The old English word "substance," implying all the resources one has at one's disposal, to include one's property and status, is probably the best translation.[49]

While others employ Hellenistic explanations for Matthew's use of διανοία, or lay out complex comparisons of the Synoptics without arriving at any substantive or helpful conclusions,[50] I agree with Birger Gerhardsson, who notes Matthew's emphasis on *attitude* throughout the Gospel. Matthew 13:22 suggests Matthew's sense of διανοία within the parable of the sower. Although Matthew does not use διανοία in this parable, he does refer to one's "*attitude* toward power and property, *the administering reason*, which either indulges in worries for resources or

---

the name Jesus somewhat roughly at 1:21, and Emmanuel at 1:23; and puns on Beelzebul at 10:25" (ibid.).

[47] Ibid.

[48] Klaus Berger, *Die Gesetzesauslegung Jesu: Ihr historischer Hintergrund im Judentum und im Alten Testament* (Neukirchen-Vluyn: Neukirchener Verlag, 1972), 209–27; cited in Gerhardsson, "Hermeneutic Program," 135; Warren Carter, *Matthew and the Margins: A Sociopolitical and Religious Reading* (Maryknoll, NY: Orbis Books, 2000), 445.

[49] Gerhardsson, "Hermeneutic Program," 136.

[50] Robert Horton Gundry, *The Use of the Old Testament in St. Matthew's Gospel* (Leiden: Brill, 1967), 23–24.

handles them with confidence." Thus, in effect, "διανοία here refers to one's 'administering' reason. By using this word instead of the object of administration (property, power), *Matthew has here made the three elements congruent*. When מאד is taken to mean *mammon*, the third element becomes somewhat incongruent with the two others."[51]

The extensive interpretation of מאד is reflected in later Jewish writings. This highest command and the question it provokes—How does one love God with one's whole heart, whole soul, and whole substance?—has invited copious midrashic writings.[52]

---

[51] Ibid. Vermes underscores Jesus' emphasis on interiority, on purity of intention, stressing primary causes of acts as lying within the heart (*Jesus and the World of Judaism*, 47–48).

[52] This interpretation of Deut 6:4 from *m. Ber.* 9:5 may have been passed down for centuries:

"With all your heart"—with your two desires, with your desire for good, and with your desire for evil.

"With all your soul"—even if He takes your soul.

"With all your might"—with all your wealth. (Or) for every measure which He metes out for you, thank him greatly. [The latter is a play on words.]

Other proto-rabbinic documents reflect similar wholehearted love for God:

"Love him with thy heart's last drop of blood, and be prepared to give up thy soul for God, if he requires it. Love him under all conditions, both in times of bliss and happiness, and in times of distress and misfortune" (*Sipre*, 73a; cf. *m. Ber.* 61b and parallels; quoted in Solomon Schechter, *Aspects of Rabbinic Theology* [New York: Schocken Books, 1961], 68, n. 1.)

"Say not, I will study the Torah with the purpose of being called Sage or Rabbi, or to acquire fortune, or to be rewarded for it in the world to come; but do it for the sake of thy love to God, though the glory will come in the end" (*Sipre* 79b; quoted in Schechter, *Aspects of Rabbinic Theology*, 68).

Finally this, from Rabbi Moses Hayyim Luzzatto, an eighteenth-century mystic: "The meaning of this love is that man should be longing and yearning after the nearness of him (God), blessed be he, and striving to reach his holiness (in the same manner) as he would pursue any object for which he feels a strong passion. He should feel that bliss and delight in mentioning his name, in uttering his praises and in occupying himself with the words of the Torah which a lover feels towards the wife of his youth, or the father towards his only son, finding delight in merely holding converse about them. . . . The man who loves his Maker with a real love requires no persuasion and inducement for his service. On the contrary, his heart will (on its own account) attract him to it. . . . This is indeed the degree (in the service of God) to be desired, to which our earlier saints, the saints of the Most High, attained to, as King David said, 'As the heart panteth after the water brooks, so panteth my soul after thee, O God. My soul thirsteth for God,

LOVE OF GOD AND LOVE OF NEIGHBOR

αὕτη ἐστὶν ἡ μεγάλη καὶ πρώτη ἐντολή.	22:38	"This is the great and first commandment.
δευτέρα δὲ ὁμοία αὐτῇ, Ἀγαπήσεις τὸν πλησίον σου ὡς σεαυτόν.	22:39	And a second is like it: 'You shall love your neighbor as yourself.'"

To love God with our whole heart, soul, and mind, Jesus declares, is the *great* commandment. Jesus repeats μεγάλη in his answer. But now he begins to expand on this response, adding that this commandment is the *first* (πρώτη) as well. Immediately, he names the *second*, which is like it. So πρώτη can mean first in order, first in importance, with priority over what is second. It can also mean first in rank or degree: foremost, most important, most prominent.[53] Both meanings apply here.

Calling this command "second" can hardly mean it is equal in importance to the "first," especially given the meaning of "first" as foremost, having highest priority. Yet Jesus concludes by saying that all the law and the prophets hang on these *two* commandments. In other words, they belong together; Jesus makes them inseparable.

The origin of the coupling of the two love commands

During the Second Temple period, these two Torah commandments were juxtaposed, in midrashic fashion, because they both began with ואהבת (you shall love): "you shall love your God" (Deut. 6:5), and "you shall love your neighbor" (or fellow human) (Lev. 19:18).[54] This juxtaposition followed the well-known *gezerah shawa* rule, which stated that "two commandments having at least one term in common were kept

---

for the living God,' and as the prophet said, 'The desire of our soul is to thy name and to the remembrance of thee' (Is. 26 8). This love must not be a love 'depending on something,' that is, that man should not love God as his benefactor, making him rich and prosperous, but it must be like the love of a son to his father, a real natural love . . . as it is said, 'Is he not thy father who has bought thee?'" (Luzzatto, מסילת ישרים [Warsaw, 1884], 27b; quoted in Schechter, *Aspects of Rabbinic Theology*, 69–70).

[53] πρῶτος, η, ον, BAGD, 725–26.

[54] In Maimonides' classic listing of the 613 commandments of the Torah, Deut. 6:5 appears as the third prescription and Lev. 19.18 as the 206th. Cf. A. H. Rabinowitz, "Commandments, The 613" in *Encyclopedia Judaica* 6:759–83; cited in Collins, "Matthew's ENTOLAI," 1342.

together, and allowed mutually to complete each other."[55] Significantly, within the entire Hebrew Bible, the consecutive form ואהבת only appears in these two commandments of love. "This verbal condition invited a combination of the commandments."[56]

So was Jesus the first to combine these love commands from the Torah? Are there other examples of this coupling?

The literary evidence tells us that, in general, the Jewish people understood Deuteronomy 6:4–9 to require reflection morning and night, and they observed this commandment in morning and evening worship rituals. Thus, few would have found surprising Jesus' quotation of Deuteronomy 6:4–5 when he was asked to name the great commandment. Furthermore, Jesus' selection of Leviticus 19:18 as a second "core" commandment was no doubt equally unsurprising. Jesus' choice of the two commandments as "great" was in keeping with the thrust of the Torah itself, which presents them as summaries. Other Jews could likely have concluded the same and would have approved Jesus' selection.

Outside the New Testament, linkage of the dual love commands is found in nonrabbinical Jewish sources: in the "Two Ways" of the *Didache*,[57] and in the *Testaments of the Twelve Patriarchs*.[58] The *Testament of Issachar* (5:2) reads: "But love the Lord and your neighbor; have compassion on the poor and weak"; the *Testament of Dan* (5:3) commands: "Love the Lord all your life and one another with a true heart." However, these documents do not designate the two as "first" or "second,"

---

[55] Gerhardsson, "Hermeneutic Program," 138.

[56] Ibid.

[57] Note that the *Didache* (100 BCE) also links the double love command with the golden rule: "First, you must love God who made you, and second, your neighbor as yourself. And whatever you want people to refrain from doing to you, you must not do to them" *Didache* 1:2, in *Early Christian Fathers*, ed. Cyril C. Richardson, Library of Christian Classics (Philadelphia: Westminster Press, 1953).

[58] Cf. *T. Zeb.* 5:1; cited in David Flusser, *Judaism and the Origins of Christianity* (Jerusalem: Magnes Press, 1988), 475, n. 7. However, there is active discussion about how much the testaments have been christianized. See Johannes Nissen, "The Distinctive Character of the New Testament Love Command in Relation to Hellenistic Judaism," in *The New Testament and Hellenistic Judaism*, ed. Peder Borgen and Søren Giversen (Aarhus, Denmark: Aarhus University Press, 1995), 125, n. 8; and Jeff T. Williams, "The Significance of Love of God and Neighbor in Luke's Gospel," chapter three of this book. See also Philo, *Spec. Laws* 2.63; cited in Carter, *Matthew and the Margins*, 445.

nor do they presume to summarize, much less epitomize, the whole of the law and the prophets.[59]

Even if the double love command was not unique to Jesus in its juxtaposition, nevertheless all evidence points to the fact that Jesus was unique in providing an emphasis on these two love commands as the center, even the essence, of the law (and the prophets).

Singular emphasis on love for neighbor

What is remarkable is that the juxtaposition of the two love commands is not found in rabbinic or proto-rabbinic literature.[60] Yet what is manifestly documented in rabbinic literature is that love of neighbor is regarded as the foundation of the entire Mosaic law. This singling out is amazing when we recall how comprehensive and detailed was the edifice of commandments by this time. During the Second Temple period, even the important notion of justice in the OT seems to have come under this rubric of neighborly love.[61] The Apostle Paul cites love of neighbor as the summary of the whole law in Romans 13:8 and Galatians 5:14.[62] This summary raises the question: Why is the Shema, with its command to love God, not mentioned more frequently in NT writings? Perhaps other virtues, such as faithfulness and obedience, were synonymous with wholehearted love for God. Not until the later writ-

---

[59] Nissen, "Distinctive Character," 128. Philo, in accordance with Hellenistic ethics, speaks of the twin virtues of "adoration and piety" (εὐσέβεια καὶ δικαιοσύνη) and of "philanthropy and righteousness" (φιλανθρωπία καὶ δικαιοσύνη). But these virtues are not expressed as commandments, nor do they refer directly to love of God or neighbor. But compare Robert Banks, *Jesus and the Law in the Synoptic Tradition* (Cambridge: Cambridge University Press, 1975), 170: "Philo declares that piety and service towards God, and philanthropy and justice towards men, are the highest commandments (*De Spec.Leg.*, II, 63; *De Abr.*, 20; *Vit.Mos.*, II, 163; et al.), and though the term 'love' is not explicitly used he undoubtedly extended the application of the second requirement to all men, not merely, as in the OT, to Jewish citizens (Lev 19.18), the resident-alien (Lev. 19.34) or, occasionally, the enemy (Exod. 23.4)."

[60] Nissen, "Distinctive Character," 127; Flusser, *Judaism and the Origins of Christianity*, 475; Gerhardsson, "Hermeneutic Program," 131.

[61] Flusser, *Judaism and the Origins of Christianity*, 475.

[62] Also James 2:8. Paul says he is free from the law, yet he is under Christ's law which, according to Romans 13, has but one provision, ἀγάπη, and we are to interpret this law by being imitators of Christ. The Sermon on the Mount is Matthew's exposition of the νόμος Χριστου (Goulder, *Midrash*, 158).

ings of the Gospels do we read explicitly about love for God (Luke 11:42; Matt. 22:37; Mark 12:30; Luke 10:27), and even there references are sparse.[63]

The bulk of NT references to love command us to love one another. Paul sums up the law as love for neighbor (Rom. 13:8–10; Gal. 5:14). So where is love for God in the NT? We are exhorted to love Christ.[64] But more common in the NT is emphasis on God's love for us, not on our love for God (e.g., 1 John 4:10–11, 19).

The overwhelming emphasis on human altruistic love in the NT and in first-century writings causes one to wonder how or why love for God and the strength of its mandate from the Shema diminished in Jewish writings during the Second Temple period, even in the NT. Was love for God so assumed, so linked with the Shema recited in daily prayers, that it would have seemed redundant to name it explicitly? Was it too nebulous to bear much discussion, too ethereal to be seen or proven, too personal to be discussed in public, too spiritual to engender much practical interest?

Love of neighbor and the golden rule

There seems to be a synonymous relationship between love of neighbor and the golden rule. As noted above, the *Didache*, an early church document dated around 100 BCE, places the golden rule alongside the double love command.[65] Matthew notably links the two together, as "the law and the prophets" (Matt. 7:12).[66] The golden rule is extant in

---

[63] Perhaps we can regard the Johannine epistles as a further development of the Synoptics. First John not only emphasizes both love commands but makes them interdependent: "If someone says, 'I love God,' and hates his brother, he is a liar; for the one who does not love his brother whom he has seen, cannot love God whom he has not seen. And this commandment we have from Him, that the one who loves God should love his brother also" (1 John 4:20–21). See Urban C. von Wahlde, *The Johannine Commandments: 1 John and the Struggle for the Johannine Tradition* (New York: Paulist Press, 1990).

[64] John 14:21, 28; 16:27; 21:15–17; 1 Cor. 16:22; 2 Cor. 2:8; Eph. 6:24; James 1:12.

[65] See n. 57.

[66] Note the different ways Matthew refers to and defines the law and the prophets. In Matt. 5:17, Jesus has come not to abolish but to fulfill the law and the prophets. In Matt. 22:40, the double love commands are regarded as the twin pegs from which hang all the law and the prophets. In Matt. 7:12, Jesus states the positive formulation of the golden rule and proclaims it to be the law and the prophets (οὗτος γάρ ἐστιν ὁ νόμος καὶ οἱ προφῆται).

both positive and negative forms,[67] and it helps us understand the implications of love of neighbor.

Which is higher, love of neighbor or love of enemy?

How does the double love command relate to the Sermon on the Mount mandate to love our enemies? Is love for neighbor related to love for enemy? How does Matthew compare or rank the two? Matthew moves from one to the other seamlessly, yet these are two fundamentally different mandates. Traditionally, a neighbor is someone from among one's own people. Even the mandated love for stranger in Leviticus 19:34 came to refer to a foreigner who had become a proselyte. The reciprocal nature of the golden rule easily complements love of neighbor. We expect such a rule in any community's standard of ethics. But Jesus' mandate to love our enemies in Matthew 5:44 is not a reciprocity ethic but a unilateral mandate.[68]

---

[67] In Palestinian Judaism, the rule is only known in negative form. The salient example is found in Talmudic tractate b. Šabb. 31a. Hillel says, "That which you hate, do not do it to your neighbour. That is the whole of the Torah; everything else is just explanation. So go and learn!" (quoted in Nissen, "Distinctive Character," 132). This statement is amazingly similar to Jesus' words in Matt. 7:12, except that he states the rule in its positive form: "Therefore, however you want people to treat you, so treat them, for this is the law and the prophets."

In Hellenistic Judaism, the rule is found in both its positive and negative form (some even combining the two). The best-known examples are found in Aristeas the Exegete, Tobit, Sirach (LXX), the Testaments of the Twelve Patriarchs and the writings of Philo (Nissen, "Distinctive Character," 132). A few examples will suffice. "What you hate, do not do to any one" (Tobit 4:15). "What a man would hate to suffer he must not do to others" (Philo, Hypothetica 7:6) (cited in E. P. Sanders, Jewish Law from Jesus to the Mishnah: Five Studies [London: SCM Press, 1990], 69–71).

[68] Hellenistic philosophy embraces the notion of love of enemies as well, although its motivation is different from that of NT paraenesis. "Non-retaliation and love of enemy are viewed as a sign of the philosopher's freedom from and superiority to the passions and illusions of the masses. A person not caught up in these passions cannot be judged" (Nissen, "Distinctive Character," 138; Nissen cites Pheme Perkins, Love Commands in the New Testament [New York: Paulist, 1982], 31). In this I see a parallel with Walter Wink's work on nonretaliation. Nissen cites further examples of enemy love from Hellenistic Jewish writings, including Joseph and Asenath, which bears striking parallels to commands in Rom. 12:17; 1 Thess. 5:15, and 1 Pet. 3:9 not to repay evil; he also cites several in Testaments of the Twelve Patriarchs (139).

In addition, Jesus contrasted the two as being different in the Sermon on the Mount. "You have heard that it was said, 'You shall love your neighbor and hate your enemy.' But I say to you, Love your enemies and pray for those who persecute you" (5:43–44; NRSV). Jesus presents the two mandates as opposites in order to dramatize his point. Does Jesus imply that love for enemy is the "higher" love? If so, why is love for neighbor coupled with love for God in Matthew 22 as the great commandment, the very essence of Torah?

John P. Meier addresses this tension by reminding us that the context of 22:34–40 is one of a controversy dialogue; hence, "the argument never rises above the horizon of the Old Testament."[69] He says that although one is tempted to treat this pericope as "the summit and summary of Jesus' moral teaching," "it is rather the summit and summary of Old Testament morality, in keeping with the question which was asked. . . . We should remember that the gospel as a whole shows us that Jesus himself, not any Old Testament command, however lofty, is the center of Christian morality."[70]

Meier's point is helpful. But let us consider this: the NT vigorously stretches the traditional concept of neighbor. Most tellingly for our purposes, Luke's parallel of our passage is not only redacted in an entirely different place in his narrative compared to its placement in Mark and Matthew, but Luke redacts it as a means to an end: to identify who is our neighbor in the parable of the good Samaritan (Luke 10:25–37). Yet Luke adds a further twist. He does not merely identify the neighbor whom we are to love; rather, Luke uses a Samaritan, the sort of foreigner hated most by Jews, as the model of how one should *be* a neighbor. The effect is sweeping. Jesus extols a hated Samaritan over two categories of respectable Jews (priest and Levite) as an example, not of whom we should love (that would combine loving one's neighbor with loving one's enemy). Rather, Jesus stretches the illustration to its breaking point by pointing to the Samaritan as the one whose actions in the parable prove that he is the best example of what it means to *be* a neighbor—although he would naturally be regarded as enemy. In other words, Jesus uses the enemy of his people to teach them how to *be* a

---

[69] John P. Meier, *The Vision of Matthew: Christ, Church, and Morality in the First Gospel* (New York: Paulist Press, 1979), 58.

[70] Ibid.

neighbor, not just to teach them whom to love.[71] While this illustration seems to stray from Matthew, it demonstrates that the notion of neighbor was becoming elastic and expansive through Jesus' teachings, bleeding into the notion of enemy without much effort.[72]

Simply put, Jesus' teachings in the NT encourage us to act like God, to be imitators of God in how we show mercy and compassion to others, not expecting a reward. Perhaps what is implied is that the more we love God, the more we are filled with God's own superabundance of love,[73] which is mercifully and generously given to friends and families, neighbors and strangers, even to enemies. Matthew feels no need to provide calculating and prescriptive words for such a dynamic of love that, ideally, knows no bounds. Matthew allows no constraints to define, delineate, categorize, or compare this ever-expanding love of God that encompasses all within its scope.

WHAT HANGS ON WHAT?

ἐν ταύταις ταῖς δυσὶν ἐντολαῖς ὅλος ὁ νόμος κρέμαται καὶ οἱ προφῆται.	22:40	"On these two commandments hang all the law and the prophets."

Up until this verse, it has been difficult to name exactly how the lawyer's question and Jesus' answer compose a test. The parallel dialogue in Mark, as mentioned, is not a test but an amicable exchange. On hearing Jesus reply with the Shema and double love commandment, the Markan scribe compliments Jesus on his correct interpretation of the law, even providing commentary on it; then Jesus commends the scribe

---

[71] See Williams, "The Significance of Love of God and Neighbor in Luke's Gospel," for a discussion of this point.

[72] Paul Ricoeur's article, "The Golden Rule," offers a creative interpretation of how to move from love of neighbor to love of enemy. He holds that the very nature of the golden rule, although it may be categorized as the *economy of gift*, nonetheless contains within it the seeds of the *logic of superabundance* that characterizes the NT. He begins one step back and notes the movement from the OT's *jus talionis*, to the golden rule, to love of enemy; he views all three as following one another in logical and spiritual flow and development. Even the differences among the three Ricoeur regards as useful in the *rhetoric of paradox*, which intentionally creates moments of disorientation in order to reorient at a higher level out of the crisis (Paul Ricoeur, "The Golden Rule: Exegetical and Theological Perplexities," *New Testament Studies* 36 (1990): 392–97.

[73] See Ricoeur, "The Golden Rule."

and offers, "You are not far from the kingdom of God" (Mark 12:29–34). From this parallel we can infer that Jesus' answer in Matthew must be equally lawful, in keeping with halakic tradition.[74] Yet Matthew embeds the entire dialogue in a controversy setting in which Jesus' authority, and his teaching authority in particular, is challenged.

But what is the test, the challenge? The question itself, apart from being characterized as a test, is legitimate, even normal for Jewish rabbinic discussions. And, as we noted, Jesus' answer is not without precedent in both Jewish and Hellenistic writings. "Jesus' answer is just the kind of answer with which no Jew would have found fault, and, in the narrative, no further question is put to him."[75] So far, the only piece that stands out as different is Jesus' naming of two love commands as joined, although one is first and one second. But both are cited in reply to the question about what is the great commandment.

The joining of these two commandments and how they are described in relation to the law and the prophets is the key to the entire passage. Jesus' concluding words in Matthew 22:40 turned upside down the understanding of the Pharisees and Jews. These scholars of the law viewed every law of the Torah, oral or written, as hanging by a strand attached to a peg, each peg a key text of scripture.[76] Jesus alludes to that common image, but he inverts it, saying, rather, that *the entire law and prophets hang by these two commands alone!* "In describing the double love commandment as something on which all the law and the prophets hang (κρέμαται), the First Evangelist was employing, no doubt consciously, a contemporary rabbinic formulation. But just as clearly, Matthew pressed this formulation into the service of an approach to the Torah markedly different from anything found among the Pharisees or rabbis."[77]

Rabbinic and proto-rabbinic literature use the Hebrew (תלה/תלא) and Aramaic (תלא), equivalents of κρεμάννυμι (to hang, either literally or figuratively); the latter being the equivalent used in the LXX as

---

[74] Sigal would agree.

[75] Margaret Davies, *Matthew* (Sheffield, England: JSOT Press, 1993), 156.

[76] Thomas G. Long, *Matthew* (Louisville, KY: Westminster John Knox Press, 1997), 255.

[77] Terence L. Donaldson, "The Law That 'Hangs' (Mt. 22:40): Rabbinic Formulation and Matthean Social World," in *Society of Biblical Literature 1990 Seminar Papers*, ed. David J. Lull (Atlanta: Scholars Press, 1990), 14.

well. And, as in Matthew 22:40, this word is used to depict some aspect of the Torah (written or oral) as being dependent on, hanging from, a written verse of the Torah. Bar Qappara asks: "What is the smallest portion of scripture from which all essential regulations of the Torah hang? 'In all your ways acknowledge him, and he will direct your paths'" (Prov. 3:6).[78]

One other example gives the literal sense of the verb within the context of its figurative use: "The rules about release from vows hover in the air and have naught to support them; the rules about the Sabbath, Festal-offerings, and Sacrilege are as mountains *hanging* by a hair, for teaching of Scripture thereon is scanty and the rules many."[79]

While Matthew broadens the meaning of "hang" beyond rabbinic tradition to include the law and the prophets, the formal similarity is clear and generally recognized.[80] This is not just a clever turn of phrase. The entire pericope reaches its fullest crescendo in this verse. Matthew has, in effect, "elevated the love commandment to the position of a canon of interpretation for the Torah as a whole."[81]

Again, nothing else about the question or Jesus' answer until now has been out of the ordinary. But Jesus' novel use of this Jewish formulation has changed everything. Interestingly, we do not know the reaction of the Pharisees to Jesus' words. We only know that at the end of the next question they are silenced for the last time in Matthew. Perhaps, on hearing Jesus' summary statement here, the words did not immediately register in their ears. Until this point, Jesus had been using familiar terms, referring to familiar ideas. Perhaps they were caught off guard by Jesus' use of "hanging," a familiar term, yet used in a sense opposite what they expected. Perhaps their minds were reeling, their tongues tied.

---

[78] b. Ber. 63a; cited in Donaldson, "The Law That 'Hangs,'" 14.

[79] m. Ḥag. 1:8; also b. Ḥag. 1:9; b. 'Erub. 8:23; cited in Donaldson, "The Law That 'Hangs,'" 14.

[80] In view of the absence of the term from early Christian usage in general and from Matthew in particular, it is quite probable that in describing the whole Torah as "hanging" on the commandments to love God and neighbor, Matthew was deliberately echoing a rabbinic formulation (see Donaldson, "The Law That 'Hangs,'" 16).

[81] Ibid., 18.

Amy Barker | 127

CONCLUSIONS

The hermeneutical function of the double love command

What was so disturbing about the way Jesus characterized the love commands was not the fact that he joined the two; the *gezerah shawah* rule allowed for this. Perhaps the Pharisees already regarded these two commandments as summary statements for the two halves of the Decalogue. We have no record of such a summary from that time period, but rabbinic tradition has offered comparable summaries of the Decalogue since then.

No, the problem was not that Jesus stated these love commands as summaries of the law. The problem was his implication—rather, his proclamation—that the whole law, even the prophets, hang or depend on—derive from and are based on—these two love commands. Whereas Mark's statement of the love commands represents an acceptable summary of the law, Matthew's statement lifts them high above all the other commands and promotes them as the basic norm, even the essence, of the law and the prophets.[82] Mark's conclusion states that no other commandment can take precedence over these two; they stand in a class by themselves. Matthew's conclusion says something different: that these two commandments are the fundamental principles on which all other scripture hangs. In so saying, Matthew eliminates any clash between these two commandments and the rest, whereas Mark recognizes such a possibility and declares how such a tension would be decided.[83]

Although Matthew's version may sound similar to Paul's summary of the law as "Love your neighbor as yourself" in Romans 13:9, the similarity is more linguistic than material. Paul seems to imply that one may dispense with the Torah if one obeys the all-inclusive mandate to love. Matthew's meaning is quite different. It is no accident that Matthew's first "law and the prophets" phrase is in 5:17: "Do not think that I have come to abolish the law or the prophets; I have come not to abolish but to fulfill"; 5:18 continues with Jesus' statement that not until heaven and earth disappear will the smallest jot or tittle disappear from the law. So within the Matthean context, where fulfillment of the

---

[82] Barth, "Matthew's Understanding," 78.

[83] Lachs, *A Rabbinic Commentary on the New Testament,* 281.

law is primary, Jesus' words in 22:40 intimate that the love commands serve as the "principle of interpretation,"[84] even the basis for reinterpreting the Torah![85] What is radical is that Matthew "endorses a *Christian casuistry* in which the command to love provides in each case the direction in which one moves when attempting to derive the particular guide for conduct from the Torah."[86] In effect, Matthew states explicitly that "the multitude of laws in Scripture are valid *inasmuch as* and *insofar as* they embody Jesus' central injunction to love God and neighbor."[87]

The law and the prophets in Matthew

An examination of the eight occurrences of νόμος (law) in Matthew[88] reveals Jesus' understanding of the law.[89] For Matthew, the law cannot be understood apart from the prophets. Matthew presents Jesus as the authoritative interpreter of the law who ensures this corrective. It is not that the law does not contain elements of love and mercy and justice; it surely does. Indeed, the prophets were those who, like Jesus, provided correctives by reminding Israel of these elements of love and mercy and justice within the Torah, even implying that these elements of mercy were more important than laws of purity and sacrifice in the holiness code (cf. Mark 12:29–34, esp. 33).[90]

---

[84] Ibid.

[85] Jack T. Sanders, *Ethics in the New Testament: Change and Development* (Philadelphia: Fortress Press, 1975),42.

[86] Ibid.

[87] Richard B. Gardner, *Matthew,* Believers Church Bible Commentary (Scottdale, PA: Herald Press, 1991), 329.

[88] 5:17, 18; 7:12; 11:13; 12:5; 22:36, 40; 23:23. This insight comes from Klyne Snodgrass, "Matthew and the Law," in *Treasures New and Old: Recent Contributions to Matthean Studies,* ed. David R. Bauer and Mark Allan Powell (Atlanta: Scholars Press, 1996), 107.

[89] In four of the references, "the law and the prophets" are joined together (5:17; 7:12; 11:13; and 22:40). In two more (5:18; 22:36), the law and the prophets are referred to in the immediate context. In the last two, the prophet Micah is quoted in response to a question or conflict concerning the law (6:6 and 6:8). More broadly, when issues concerning the law are the subject of debate, a word from the prophets is brought to bear: Matt. 15:1–2 refers to Isa. 29:13; Matt. 21:13 to Isa. 56:7 and Jer. 7:11. Additionally, the Pharisees are told that their application of the law is not in keeping with the prophetic view in Matt. 23:29–36, and are therefore accused of being lawless (v. 28).

[90] This is Marcus J. Borg's argument in *Conflict, Holiness and Politics in the Teaching of Jesus* (New York: Edwin Mellen, 1984), 123, 128. It is no stretch to broaden, or interpret, Mat-

The radical hermeneutic of Matthew's Jesus

While Jesus did not do away with the purity laws, he clearly regarded them as secondary to mercy. One need only read Matthew 8–9, in which Jesus violates these laws by deliberately touching a leper, a hemorrhaging woman, and a dead girl; he also enters the house of a Gentile. And he pointedly disregards cleanliness regulations in 15:1–20. It is apparent that Jesus regards these concerns as unimportant in light of the demand for love and mercy, which is his key to understanding the law and the prophets. In fact, one could say that "mercy" in Matthew may connote the golden rule and love for both neighbor and enemy.

This observation only underscores our interpretation that Matthew 22:40 is radical. There is no mistake in Jesus' shocking wording.[91] The double love command is put forward as both the central element of the law and the hermeneutical key for correctly interpreting its individual demands."[92]

When we apply this hermeneutical key to the rest of Matthew, we can better understand Matthew's Gospel. For example, only Matthew adds love for neighbor at the end of the list of Decalogue commands (signifying its greater importance, even its summary effect) required for eternal life (19:18–19; cf. Mark 10:19 and Luke 18:20). Matthew's entire hermeneutic is based on interpreting all the law and the prophets through, and by means of, the double love command (in its fullest

---

thew's use of ἀγάπη to include mercy. Hosea 6:6 and 6:8 are already mentioned above. In Matt. 23:23, justice, mercy, and faithfulness are elevated as the weightier matters of the law. In Matt. 5:7 the merciful are promised mercy; in Matt. 18:33 the point of the parable of the unforgiving servant is that the mercy of God requires that people show mercy to each other (Snodgrass, "Matthew and the Law," 109).

[91] According to Schechter, the Pentateuch was put on a higher level than the prophets. Moses' vision was regarded as more clear than that of his successors (*Yebam.* 49b; *Lev. R.* 1), although there was not usually any contradiction perceived between the Pentateuch and the prophets (Schechter, *Aspects of Rabbinic Theology*, 118–19). It is also true that *Torah* developed a broader meaning, to include the prophets and the hagiographa. "To the Jew . . . the term *Torah* implied a teaching or instruction, and was therefore wide enough to embrace the whole of the Scriptures" (ibid., 124–25).

[92] Sim, *Matthew*, 127–28. Also see Snodgrass, "Matthew and the Law," 107–110; J. Andrew Overman, *Matthew's Gospel and Formative Judaism: The Social World of the Matthean Community* (Minneapolis: Fortress Press, 1990), 85; Saldarini, *Matthew's Christian-Jewish Community*, 161–63; and Dan O. Via, Jr., *Self-Deception and Wholeness in Paul and Matthew* (Minneapolis: Fortress Press, 1990), 83–84.

connotation of love and mercy).[93] "To the question 'What is the law?' the answer is, 'The love command and the demand for mercy.' To the question, 'When is the law not law?' the answer is, 'When it is only law and not in keeping with the tenor of all the law and the prophets.'"[94]

The reciprocal nature of love for God and love for neighbor

Patte argues that the Pharisees and Sadducees are depicted in Matthew as misconstruing the relationship between God and human beings, regarding each as occupying a realm separate from the other that cannot be breached.[95] Jesus' double love command with its hermeneutical import cannot allow such a separation (see Matt. 25:31–46). Although love for God retains priority, Jesus places the two love commands alongside each other to show that they are not far apart, even that they are interdependent and interrelated. Just as our neighbor (πλήσιον) is near, so is God near to us (cf. Rom 10:8–9). Our relationship with God affects our relationship with our neighbor, for good or ill. First John says that this statement (I John 4:19–21) and the reverse (I John 4:7–8) are both true.

The reciprocal nature of the two love commands can be deduced from Jesus' words in Matthew 5:23–26, in which one who brings to the altar a gift for sacrifice to God must first go and be reconciled with his sister or brother. "Thus there can be no obedience towards God in a vacuum, as it were, no obedience apart from the concrete situation in which I stand as a human being among others."[96]

However, this reciprocal relationship between love for God and love for people should not be automatically equated, as if one implies and embraces the whole of the other. "It would be wrong to equate love for God narrowly with the manifestation of love for one's neighbor."[97]

---

[93] Patte, *Matthew*, 74, 167–68; Borg, *Conflict, Holiness and Politics in the Teaching of Jesus*, 71, 161.

[94] Snodgrass, "Matthew and the Law," 111.

[95] Patte, *Matthew*, 315. We know that love of God and the other were often juxtaposed and evenly stressed in Second Temple Judaism. See the discussion in Williams, "The Significance of Love of God and Neighbor in Luke's Gospel."

[96] Rudolf Schnackenburg, *The Moral Teaching of the New Testament* (New York: Seabury Press, 1965), 98 (citing Rudolf Bultmann, *Jesus* [Tübingen: J. C. B. Mohr (Paul Siebeck), 1951], 99).

[97] Ibid, 99. However, see Williams' discussion of the the "single command" in Luke.

The life and teachings of Jesus manifest his love for and dependence on God, his Father. Jesus exhibits, on the foundation of his resolute love for God, both love for neighbor and love for enemy.[98]

Matthew's hermeneutic: The double love command

I find convincing Gerhardsson's view that Matthew 22:37–40 is a succinct construal of Matthew's entire hermeneutic program. This paper cannot do justice to Gerhardsson's work; a few examples must suffice.

1. Jesus' fulfillment of the law and the prophets (Matt. 5:17) brings about the superior righteousness Matthew espouses (Matt. 5:20). This righteousness is made possible only through and with the help of the first and great commandment: to love God with one's entire heart, soul, and mind. "Several examples are given in the Sermon concerning how the commandments in the old law must be interpreted as if they were 'dependent' upon the greatest and first commandment. This commandment need not be quoted; it is allowed to play its steering, deepening, and widening role under the surface."[99]

2. Leviticus 19:18 serves a governing function in the Sermon on the Mount. None of the commandments used as examples are commands regarding rituals, food, or purity. All the examples used from the law concern relations toward one's neighbor. In all cases, Jesus' interpretation of the commandments "presents an attitude towards life that is beneficial towards one's fellow man."[100]

3. Gerhardsson's most intriguing observation, pertinent to this paper, is that all the OT quotations introduced in Matthew 5:17–48 employ the verb ἀκούειν (to hear); e.g., "You have *heard* that it has been said to those of ancient times . . ."

---

[98] Jesus' ministry and teachings demonstrate the fulfillment of the entire context of Leviticus 19. He countered the religious elite's practices that were oppressive; he healed the sick (4:23–24); he upheld the commands to honor parents, not steal and not bear false witness (19:18–19); he forbade oaths (5:33–37) and revenge (5:38–42). He extended the command to love one's neighbor to praying for one's enemies (5:43–46), and even to selling one's possessions to give to the poor (Matt. 19:19–21; cf. 6:24).

[99] Gerhardsson, "Hermeneutic Program," 143.

[100] Ibid.

Working from the old, Jesus introduces the new: "But I say unto you . . ." Jesus' authoritative words radicalize and total-ize the commandments quoted, again emphasizing love for both neighbor and enemy. Matthew alone concludes that it is by obeying and living these radically new commands that we can be perfect as our heavenly Father is perfect.[101]

Although it is not explicitly written as preface to the command to love God in Matthew 22:37 (as is the case in Deut. 6:4–5), the Shema pervades Matthew. Not only does Matthew teach Israel how to regard the law, using the double love command hermeneutic; he teaches Israel how to *hear*: how to hear God, how to hear God's word. The OT prophets' emphasis on Israel's inability to hear is a predominant theme picked up in the NT, inferring that Israel did not hear in the right way.[102] Mat-thew's Jesus teaches and demonstrates exactly how Israel is to *hear* (*shema*) YHWH their God. Simply put, a life lived in accordance with the double love command signifies that one has learned how to hear God.

The parable of the sower (Matt. 13:3–23) is illustrative of how the Shema and its love command underlies Jesus' teachings in Matthew. Alluding to Isaiah's prophecy about those who do not hear (Isa. 6:9–10), Jesus composes a parable that explains how God's people have failed to hear because of their failure to love God wholly. Three categories of hearers do not fully hear the word; the fourth category does hear and receives rewards in three categories. But why four categories, when this parable simply contrasts those who hear with those who do not hear? Why not two categories?

Those who have a hardened heart, who do not love God with their whole heart, are the hardened path, from whom the evil one easily snatches away the message of the kingdom. Those who fall away under

---

[101] This is not to say that Jesus' application of the law was different from those offered by his contemporaries. He, like Hillel, adapted the law to human need. Luke's rough parallel substitutes "merciful" for perfect (6:36). The only other time Matthew uses "perfect" (τέλειος) is, coincidentally, in Matt. 19:21. After Jesus concludes his listing of the Decalogue commandments with the love-for-neighbor command, and the young man says he has kept all of these, Jesus provides commentary and application for how this man should love his neighbor: "If you wish to be *perfect,* go and sell your posses-sions . . ."

[102] Isa. 6:9 remains an indictment in the NT: Matt. 13:14–15; Luke 8:10; John 12:40; Acts 28:26–27; Rom 11:8.

pressure of trouble or persecution to save their own life ("soul") do not love with God with whole soul; they are the rocky, shallow soil. Those who allow worries and *mammon* to stifle the word do not love God with their whole substance; these are the plants choked by thorns. But those who *hear* in the right way, and who understand the word, bear fruit in three categories:[103] thirtyfold, sixtyfold, and a hundredfold.[104] In other words, if we don't love God with all three faculties of Deuteronomy 6:4, we do not hear *(shema)* God.

In Gerhardsson's creative interpretation of Deuteronomy 6:4–5, Matthew's Jesus holds together, in tension, the old and the new. While the parable of the wineskins appears in all three Synoptics, only Matthew is interested in preserving the old with the new (9:17). The past revelation of God's will is given a new understanding in Jesus. Matthew refuses to regard the former as wrong; he regards the latter as its fulfillment.[105]

Fulfillment is the key to Matthew's reconciliation of the old with the new—the law and the prophets with Jesus Christ. Perfection results when one *hears* well enough to love God and love one another and so fulfill the law and the prophets, as Jesus did.

And love—love for God and love for one's fellow human beings—is the summary and summit, the heart and the marrow, the source and goal of all. Upon this love—love for God and love for neighbor—everything else hangs, even and especially the law and the prophets. Matthew's double love command brings us, ultimately, to the person of Jesus Christ, the one who perfectly fulfills the law and the prophets because he perfectly embodies love for God and love for humanity.

---

[103] Again the number three is a subtle Hebraic play on the three modes of loving God that demonstrate the full hearing of God that results in the fullest loving of God.

[104] Ibid, 144.

[105] Ivor Jones, "Matthew" in *Early Christian Thought in its Jewish Context*, ed. John Barclay and John Sweet (Cambridge: Cambridge University Press, 1996), 59.

Acknowledgements

I want to express my thanks to Institute of Mennonite Studies for accepting this project. This generous action affirmed the scholarship of the contributors and gave their work added importance. It was a privilege to have the biblical studies seminar as part of my teaching load. The editors at IMS have taken great care with the manuscript and this often thankless task is gratefully acknowledged. I would also like to thank Mary Klassen for overseeing the book's design. Finally, I wish to thank Paul Keim for his generous preface.

Contributors

Paul Keim is professor of Bible and religion at Goshen College, Goshen, Indiana.

Perry B. Yoder is professor emeritus of Old Testament, Associated Mennonite Biblical Seminary, Elkhart, Indiana.

Jackie A. Wyse is engaged in urban mission work in Almere, the Netherlands, under the auspices of Mennonite Mission Network and the Dutch Mennonite committees for mission, peace, and relief work.

James W. Carlson is a PhD student at Fuller Theological Seminary, Pasadena, California, with a concentration in New Testament.

Jeff T. Williams is the associate pastor at Nappanee Brethren in Christ church, Nappanee, Indiana.

Amy Barker is campus pastor and assistant professor of youth ministry at Bethel College, North Newton, Kansas.